Letters Home

James B. Rieley

In war, there are no unwounded soldiers.

Jose Narosky

In an age like ours, which is not given to letter-writing,
we forget
what an important part it used to play in people's lives.

Anatole Broyard

Letters Home

4

Table of Contents

At the outbreak of the Civil War in 1861, in response to a call to arms by President Lincoln, Ohio raised 23 volunteer infantry regiments for three months' service, 10 more regiments than the state's quota. When it became evident that the war would not end quickly, Ohio began raising regiments for three-year terms of enlistment. At first the majority were stocked with eager volunteers and recruits. Two of these volunteers were the Rieley brothers from Cleveland.

I can't remember when I first heard about the Civil War, or even when I found out that my father's grandfather and his brother were in the war. But I can remember when I first became aware of the fact that my family was in possession of the actual letters that the two brothers had written home during their time in service. Before my father passed away in 1974, I had seen copies of some of these letters and eventually received copies of my own. For years I kept the letters to pass along to my sons at some point, but several years ago, I was talking to a friend in London and told him about the letters. He inspired me to share the letters in a book format.

The Rieley family came from Ireland, with the father Hugh Rieley coming from County Cavan, and his wife Margaret Owen coming from Monaghan County. After immigrating to the United States in the early 1800's, they eventually settled in Cleveland, Ohio. Mary Ann Rieley, the eldest of the siblings, was born in 1839. John Rieley was born in 1840; Frank in 1842; William in 1847; Hugh in 1850; Thomas in 1853; and Edwin (Sylvester) in 1855. The letters contained in this book were written by John and Frank, with most of them being sent to their Mother and Sister.

To put some context to all this, John Rieley was my Great Grandfather. He and his wife (Anna Haller) had three children; John Frank Rieley (1908 – 1974), Jean Theresa Rieley (1915 – 1964), and Margaret Ann Rieley (1917 – 2005) My father was John Frank Rieley, the grandson of John Rieley.

And just a few side notes about the actual letters: Some of the letters contain references to what apparently were questions or statements in letters the brothers received from their family, but sadly those letters had not been saved.

As you will see in some of the letters, the language used would be deemed to be highly inappropriate today, but in the mid-1860's, the United States was a completely different cultural environment than it is today.

You will also see that occasionally, the spelling of names, as well as the names themselves, appear to be different. Frank Rieley was born Francis Rieley, but for most of his correspondence home used Frank as his name. The spelling of Rieley appears in different variations on army documents, and in other family records I either have or have seen. No explanation is available for this, other than the documents were written by someone else, and all the variations do sound the same. It was the 1860's.

Re-writing all the letters that had been sent home by the brothers has been quite a challenge, both for me and for my computer's word processing software. Whilst there are some of the letters (quite a few actually) that appear to have typographical errors, the reality is that this is the way they were written by the brothers. I have endeavoured to faithfully reproduce the content and the formatting of way in which they were written at the time.

James B Rieley

Acknowledgements

This book would have been impossible to consider doing without the efforts and support of several people.

My Aunt, Margaret Ann (Peg) Rieley Dennis, was the one who, as an avid devotee of family history, collected and did the original typing of the letters from their hand-written, and often difficult to understand, form. In her later years, Peg donated the actual letters from Frank and John Rieley to the Western Reserve Historical Society Library (Cleveland, Ohio), where they now are.

Suzanne Foster, my friend. Sue Foster was the best friend of my Aunt Peg and now probably the most authoritative source of information about my family...and a very special person whom I consider to be part of my family.

Elizabeth Ann (Betsy) Rieley Troth, a grand-daughter of Thomas Rieley, who had shared with me the wealth of information she has about the history of the Rieley family.

Jimmy Wales, who with Larry Sanger, co-founded Wikipedia, for providing relatively easy access to many of the footnotes and much of the historical research that went into the preparation of this book.

Nicholas Watkis, a good friend who provided the encouragement to write this record of my relatives service during the Civil War.

Glossary

During my time transcribing all the letters, I sometimes came upon a word or phrase that caused me to stop and Google in order to better understand what the brothers were referring too. Because of that, I thought that you might feel the need to do the same, so I found a rather brilliant website called "Glossary of Civil War Terms" online *(http://www.civilwar.org/education/history/glossary/glossary.html)* and have copied some of its contents here for you. In addition, I have added footnotes to help make clear what was written in the letters from Frank and John Rieley.

Abatis: (pronounced *ab-uh-tee, ab-uh-tis, uh-bat-ee*, or *uh-bat-is*) A line of trees, chopped down and placed with their branches facing the enemy, used to strengthen fortifications.

Abolitionist: Someone who wishes to abolish or get rid of slavery.

Agriculture: The science of growing crops or raising livestock; farming.

Aide-de-Camp: A soldier who was appointed by an officer to be his confidential assistant. The aide wrote and delivered orders and held a position of responsibility which required him to know troop positions and where officer quarters were located. The aide-de-camp was an officer by virtue of his position and he took orders from his commander only.

Ambulance: A two-wheeled or four-wheeled wagon or cart used to transport wounded or sick soldiers.

Ambush: To lie in wait for an unexpected attack.

Antebellum: (pronounced *an-tee-bel-uhm*) A term often used to describe the United States of America before the outbreak of the Civil War.

Armory: A place where weapons and other military supplies are manufactured.

Army: The largest organizational group of soldiers, made up of one or more corps. There were 16 Union armies (named after rivers, such as the Army of the Potomac) and 23 Confederate armies (named after states or regions, such as the Army of Northern Virginia). 1 company = 50 to 100 men, 10 companies = 1 regiment, about 4 regiments = 1 brigade, 2 to 5 brigades = 1 division, 2 or more divisions = 1 corps, 1 or more corps = 1 army.

Arsenal: A place where weapons and other military supplies are stored.

Artillery: Cannon or other large caliber firearms; a branch of the army armed with cannon.

Barbette: Raised platform or mound allowing an artillery piece to be fired over a fortification's walls without exposing the gun crew to enemy fire.

Barrel: The long metal tube on a gun through which a projectile is fired.

Battery: The basic unit of soldiers in an artillery regiment; similar to a company in an infantry regiment. Batteries included 6 cannon (with the horses, ammunition, and equipment needed to move and fire them), 155 men, a captain, 30 other officers, 2 buglers, 52 drivers, and 70 cannoneers. As the War dragged on, very few batteries fought at full strength. A battery can also be the position on a battlefield where cannon are located.

Bayonet: (pronounced *bay-uh-net*) A metal blade, like a long knife or short sword, that could be attached to the end of a musket or rifle-musket and used as a spear or pike in hand-to-hand combat.

Bedroll: Blanket or other bedding rolled up and carried over the shoulder by a soldier. Sometimes soldiers would include personal belongings in their bedroll.

Bivouac: (*pronounced BIH-voo-ack*) Temporary soldier encampment in which soldiers were provided no shelter other than what could be assembled quickly, such as branches; sleeping in the open.

Blockade: The effort by the North to keep ships from entering or leaving Southern ports.

Bombproof: A field fortification which was made to absorb the shock of artillery strikes. It was constructed of heavy timbers and its roof was covered with soil.

"Bonnie Blue Flag": Extremely popular Confederate song named after the first flag of the Confederacy, which had one white star on a blue background. The lyrics listed each state in the order in which they seceded from the Union.

Border States: The states of Maryland, Delaware, Kentucky, and Missouri. Although these states did not officially join the Confederacy, many of their citizens supported the South.

Breach: A large gap or "hole" in a fortification's walls or embankments caused by artillery or mines, exposing the inside of the fortification to assault.

Breastworks: Barriers which were about breast-high and protected soldiers from enemy fire.

Breech-loading: Rifle-muskets that could be loaded at the breech (in the middle between the barrel and the stock) instead of from the end (by shoving gunpowder and a ball down the barrel) were called breech-loading guns.

Brevet: (pronounced *brehv-it*) An honorary promotion in rank, usually for merit. Officers did not usually function at or receive pay for their brevet rank.

Brigade: A large group of soldiers usually led by a brigadier general. A brigade was made of four to six regiments. 1 company = 50 to 100 men, 10 companies = 1 regiment, about 4 regiments = 1 brigade, 2 to 5 brigades = 1 division, 2 or more divisions = 1 corps, 1 or more corps = 1 army.

Brogan: A leather shoe, similar to an ankle-high boot, issued to soldiers during the Civil War. Brogans were also popular amongst civilians during the time period.

Bummer: A term used to describe marauding or foraging soldiers. Although armies on both sides often had rules against foraging or stealing from private residences, some soldiers often found ways to do so.

Butternut: Home-made dye used to color "homespun" cloth a yellow-brown color, used when imported gray cloth became scarce. The dye was made from the husks, leaves, bark, branches and/or roots of butternut and walnut trees. "Butternut" was also a slang term for a Confederate soldier.

Caisson: (pronounced *kay-suhn*) – A two-wheeled cart that carried two ammunition chests, tools, and a spare wheel for artillery pieces. The caisson could be attached to a limber, which would allow both to be pulled by a team of horses.

Caliber: The distance around the inside of a gun barrel measured in thousands of an inch. Bullets are labeled by what caliber gun they fit. **Campaign**: A series of military operations that form a distinct phase of the War (such as the Shenandoah Valley Campaign).

Canister: A projectile, shot from a cannon, filled with about 35 iron balls the size of marbles that scattered like the pellets of a shotgun.

Canteen: Round container used to carry water; made of wood or tin and carried over the shoulder by a strap.

Cap: Essential to firing a percussion rifle-musket, a cap is a tiny brass shell that holds fulminate of mercury. The cap is placed on the gun so that when a trigger is pulled, the hammer falls on the cap. The chemical in the cap ignites and flame shoots into the chamber that holds the gunpowder. This ignites the powder and the blast shoots the bullet out of the barrel.

Carbine: A breech-loading, single-shot, rifle-barreled gun primarily used by cavalry troops. A carbine's barrel is several inches shorter than a regular rifle-musket.

Cartridge: Roll of thin paper which held a small amount of gun powder in the bottom and a ball or bullet in the top. A soldier needed to tear off the top of the cartridge in order to fire his weapon - part of the nine steps to fire a muzzle loading gun (or five to fire a breech loading gun).

Casemate: (pronounced *kays-mayt*) A sturdily-built, arched masonry chamber enclosed by a fortification's ramparts or walls. Casemates were often used to protect gun positions, powder magazines, storerooms or living quarters.

Cash Crop: A crop such as tobacco or cotton which was grown to be sold for cash --not grown for food like corn or wheat.

Casualty: A soldier who was wounded, killed, or missing in action.

Cavalry: A branch of the military mounted on horseback. Cavalry units in the Civil War could move quickly from place to place or go on scouting expeditions on horseback, but usually fought on foot. Their main job was to gather information about enemy movements. Until the spring of 1863, the Confederate cavalry force was far superior to its Federal counterpart.

Charge: To rush towards the enemy.

Chevaux-de-Frise: (pronounced *sheh-VOH-de-freez*) A defensive obstacle constructed by using a long horizontal beam pierced with diagonal rows of sharpened spikes. When several cheval-de-frise (singular, pronounced *she-VAL-de-freez*) were bolted together they created an effective barrier for roads and fortifications.

Colors: A flag identifying a regiment or army. The "Color Bearer" was the soldier who carried the flag in battle, which was considered a great honor.

Columbiad: (*pronounced cull-UHM-bee-ad*) Smoothbore heavy artillery which lobbed shot and shell; used in coastal fortifications. By the end of the Civil War, the columbiad was rendered obsolete by rifled, banded artillery.

Commutation: Stipulation adopted by both the Union and Confederate governments which allowed certain draftees to pay a fee in order to avoid military service. Because the fee was higher than the average worker's annual salary, this provision angered less-wealthy citizens on both sides of the war.

Company: A group of 50 to 100 soldiers led by a captain. 10 companies = 1 regiment, about 4 regiments = 1 brigade, 2 to 5 brigades = 1 division, 2 or more divisions = 1 corps, 1 or more corps = 1 army.

Confederacy: Also called the South or the Confederate States of America, the Confederacy incorporated the states that seceded from the United States of America to form their own nation. Confederate states were: Alabama, Arkansas, Florida, Georgia, Louisiana, Mississippi, North Carolina, South Carolina, Tennessee, Texas, and Virginia.

Confederate: Loyal to the Confederacy. Also Southern or Rebel.

Conscript: A draftee. The military draft became a necessity on both sides of the conflict. While many conscripts were excellent soldiers, veterans often considered draftees to be inferior, unreliable soldiers. Towns often posted pleas for volunteers in order to "avoid the draft".

Contrabands: Escaped slaves who fled to the Union lines for protection.

Copperhead: Term for a Northerner who opposed the war effort.

Corps: (pronounced *kohr* or *korz*) A very large group of soldiers led by (Union) a major general or (Confederate) a lieutenant general and designated by Roman numerals (such as XI Corps). Confederate corps were often called by the name of their commanding general (as in Jackson's Corps). 1 company = 50 to 100 men, 10 companies = 1 regiment, about 4 regiments = 1 brigade, 2 to 5 brigades = 1 division, 2 or more divisions = 1 corps, 1 or more corps = 1 army.

Cotton-Clad: Gunboats using stacked cotton bales to protect themselves from enemy fire.

Coup de Main: (pronounced *koo-duh-mahn*) A French term used to describe a quick, vigorous attack that surprises the enemy.

Courier: (pronounced *KUHR-ee-er*) A soldier who served the officers of his regiment by carrying mail or messages.

Dahlgren Guns: Bronze boat howitzers and rifles used by the navies which were useful in river operations. They were named after Admiral John A. Dahlgren, their inventor.

Defeat in Detail: Defeating a military force unit by unit. This occurred when units were unable to support one another, often because of distance.

Defensive: Resisting or protecting against attack from someone.

Defilade: (pronounced *DEH-fih-lade*) To arrange walls, embankments and other features of a fortification or field work so that the enemy cannot make an accurate shot inside.

Democratic Party: The major political party in America most sympathetic to states rights and willing to tolerate the spread of slavery to the territories. Democrats opposed a strong Federal government. Most Southern men were Democrats before the War.

Demonstration: A military movement which is used to draw the enemy's attention, distracting the enemy so that an attack can be made in another location.

Drill: To practice marching, military formations and the steps in firing and handling one's weapon.

Dropsy: (pronounced *drop-see*) Nineteenth-century term for the condition known today as edema. Fluid builds up in the tissues and causes limbs to swell up horribly.

Dysentery: (pronounced *DISS-ehn-terr-ee*) Intestinal disease causing severe diarrhea. Dysentery was a leading cause of deaths by disease.

Earthwork: A field fortification (such as a trench or a mound) made of earth. Earthworks were used to protect troops during battles or sieges, to protect artillery batteries, and to slow an advancing enemy.

Emancipation: Freedom from slavery.

Enfilade: (pronounced *en-fuh-leyd*) To fire along the length of an enemy's battle line.

Entrenchments: Long cuts (trenches) dug out of the earth with the dirt piled up into a mound in front; used for defense.

Fascine: (pronounced *fah-seen*) A tightly bound bundle of straight sticks used to reinforce earthworks, trenches or lunettes. Fascines could also be used to make revetments, field magazines, fill material and blinds.

Federal: Loyal to the government of the United States. Also known as Union, Yankee, or Northern.

Feint: (pronounced *feynt*) To pretend to attack in one direction while the real attack is directed somewhere else.

Fieldworks: Temporary fortifications put up by an army in the field.

Flank: Used as a noun, a "flank" is the end (or side) of a military position, also called a "wing". An unprotected flank is "in the air", while a protected flank is a "refused flank". Used as a verb, "to flank" is to move around and gain the side of an enemy position, avoiding a frontal assault.

Flying Battery: A system where several horse-drawn cannons would ride along the battle front, stop and set up the guns, fire, limber up, and ride to another position. This practice gave the impression that many guns were in use when only a few were actually being used.

Foraging: A term used for "living off the land," as well as plundering committed by soldiers.

Fortification: Something that makes a defensive position stronger, like high mounds of earth to protect cannon or spiky breastworks to slow an enemy charge. Fortifications may be man-made structures or a part of the natural terrain. Man-made fortifications could be permanent (mortar or stone) or temporary (wood and soil). Natural fortifications could include waterways, forests, hills and mountains, swamps and marshes.

Furlough: A leave from duty, granted by a superior officer. The furloughed soldier carried papers which described his appearance, his unit, when he left and when he was due to return. Furlough papers also contained a warning that failure to return on time would cause the soldier to be "considered a deserter".

Gabions: (pronounced *gey-bee-en*) Cylindrical wicker baskets which were filled with rocks and dirt, often used to build field fortifications or temporary fortified positions.

Garrison: A group of soldiers stationed at a military post.

Goober Pea: A common Southern term for "peanut".

"Graybacks": A slang term for lice, or occasionally an offensive "Yankee" slang term for Confederate soldiers.

Greenbacks: Paper currency which began to circulate in the North after February 1862 with the passage of the Legal Tender Act. The bills were called "greenbacks" because of their color.**Green Troops**: Phrase used to describe soldiers who were either new to the military or had never fought in a battle before.

Hardtack: Hardtack is a term used to describe the hard crackers often issued to soldiers of both sides during the Civil War. These crackers consisted of nothing more than flour, water, and salt. They were simple and inexpensive to make in very large quantities. However, these crackers became almost rock solid once they went stale.

Havelock: (pronounced *hav-loc*) A white cloth cover that went over a soldier's kepi, and had a long back that covered a soldier's neck and shoulders. Although it saw use in the early stages of the war, soldiers quickly learned that it cut off circulation around the head and face, leading to the eventual abandonment of the havelock.

Haversack: Small canvas bag, about one foot square, used to carry a soldier's food. Typically, these bags were painted with black tar to make them waterproof.

Housewife: Small sewing kit soldiers used to repair their garments.

Howitzer: A cannon which fired hollow projectiles and was generally lighter and shorter than its solid-shot cousins. A howitzer's projectiles had a smaller powder charge. Also, canister projectiles contained more small balls than other types of canister. Howitzers were useful in defending fortifications and causing disorder within with in an attacking force.

(Attack) In Detail: To destroy the enemy piece by piece — by attacking smaller segments one at a time — instead of attacking the entire force all at once.**Indian Territory**: The area that is now Oklahoma (except for the panhandle.)

Industry: Manufacturing goods from raw materials, such as cloth from cotton or machine parts from iron.

Infantry: A branch of the military in which soldiers traveled and fought on foot.

"Infernal Machine": A term of contempt for torpedoes (either the land or the water variety). This term was also used to describe the Confederate vessel *H.L. Hunley* - the first successful submarine.

Instant: Used in letters and reports, "instant" referred to a particular day in the same month. For example, Robert E. **Lee's Report Concerning the Attack at Harpers Ferry**, written on October 19, 1859, states that Lee arrived on the "night of the 17th instant". The "17th instant" would be October 17th.

Insult: A sudden, open, unconcealed attack upon a fortified position with the intent of capturing it before its defenders could mount an effective defense.

Interior Lines: A military strategy which holds that the fastest, most efficient maneuvers, transportation and communication are conducted within an enclosed geographic area as opposed to outside the geographic area.

Ironclad: A ship protected by iron armor.

Juggernaut: (pronounced *juhg-er-nawt*) An overwhelming, advancing force that crushes or seems to crush everything in its path.

Kepi: (pronounced *KEH-peeh*) Cap worn by Civil War soldiers; more prevalent among Union soldiers.

Limber: A two-wheeled cart that carried one ammunition chest for an artillery piece. The artillery piece could be attached to the limber, which would allow both to be pulled by a team of horses. Also verb: The practice of attaching a piece of artillery to the limber that holds its ammunition.

Litter: A stretcher which was carried by two people and used to transport wounded soldiers.

Long Roll: A long, continuous drum call which commanded a regiment to assemble.

"Lost Cause": Cultural movement in which Southern states attempted to cope - mentally and emotionally - with devastating defeat and Northern military occupation after the Civil War. The movement idealized life in the antebellum South, loudly protested against Reconstruction policies, and exalted Confederate figures such as "Stonewall" Jackson and Robert E. Lee.

Lunette: (pronounced *loo-net*) A fortification shaped roughly like a half-moon. It presented two or three sides to the enemy but the rear was open to friendly lines.

Mason-Dixon line: A boundary surveyed in the 1760s that ran between Pennsylvania to the North and Delaware, Maryland and (West) Virginia to the South. It became a symbolic division between free states and slave states.

Massacre The cruel killing of a number of helpless or unresisting people.

Magazine: A fortified location where powder or supplies were stored.

Militia: Troops, like the National Guard, who are only called out to defend the land in an emergency.

Minie Bullet (or minié bullet): (pronounced *min-ee* or *min-ee-ay*) The standard infantry bullet of the Civil War. The bullet was designed for muzzle-loading rifle-muskets. It was invented by two Frenchmen, Henri-Gustave Delvigne and Claude-Étienne Minié (pronounced "*min-ee-ay*"). It was small enough to load quickly, and had a special feature that let it take advantage of a rifled-barrel. When the rifle-musket was fired, expanding gas from the gunpowder blast was caught in the hollow base of the bullet forcing it against the rifled grooves inside the barrel.

Monitor: Originally, the *U.S.S. Monitor*, the first ironclad warship in the United States Navy, commanded by **Admiral John L. Worden**. The vessel had a large, round gun turret on top of a flat raft-like bottom, which caused some spectators to describe it as a "cheesebox on a raft". The first engagement between ironclads occurred on March 8-9, 1862, **at the Battle of**

Hampton Roads, VA, when the *U.S.S. Monitor* fought the *C.S.S. Virginia* (formerly the *U.S.S. Merrimack*). Eventually a "monitor" became the official term for an entire class of warships modeled after the original *U.S.S. Monitor*.

Mortar: An unrifled artillery gun which was designed to launch shells over walls and enemy fortifications. The most famous Civil War mortar is the "Dictator" -- a mortar which was mounted on a railroad car and used during the siege of Petersburg. With its 13 inch bore it was capable of launching two hundred pound shells.

Musket: A smoothbore firearm fired from the shoulder. Thrust from exploding powder shoots the bullet forward like a chest pass in basketball.

Muster: To formally enroll in the army or to call roll.

Muzzle-loading: Muzzle-loading muskets or rifle muskets had to be loaded from the end by putting the gunpowder and the bullet or ball down the barrel.

Napoleon Gun: Another name for the Model 1857 gun howitzer. This lighter, more maneuverable field artillery piece fired 12 pound projectiles and was very popular with both Federal and Confederate armies.

Napoleonic Tactics: The tactics used by Napoleon Bonaparte that were studied by military men and cadets at West Point before the Civil War. His tactics were brilliant for the technology of warfare at the time he was fighting. However, by the Civil War, weapons had longer ranges and were more accurate than they had been in Napoleon's day. **Navy**: A branch of the military using ships to conduct warfare. During the Civil War, "blue water" ships cruised the oceans and "brown water" boats floated up and down the rivers.

Nom-de-guerre: (pronounced *nahm-duh-gair*) Literally, in French this means "war name". A nom-de-guerre is a nickname earned in battle, such as "Stonewall" Jackson or "Fighting Joe" Hooker.

North: Also called the Union or the United States the North was the part of the country that remained loyal to the Federal government during the Civil War. Northern states were: Connecticut, Delaware, Illinois, Indiana, Iowa, Kansas, Maine, Massachusetts, Michigan, Minnesota, New Hampshire, New Jersey, New York, Ohio, Pennsylvania, Rhode Island, Vermont, and Wisconsin. West Virginia became a Northern state in 1863 and California and Oregon were also officially Northern but they had little direct involvement in the War.

Offensive: Actively attacking someone.

Ordnance: The term used for military supplies, such as weaponry and ammunition.

Parole: A pledge by a prisoner of war or a defeated soldier not to bear arms. When prisoners were returned to their own side during the War (in exchange for men their side had captured) the parole was no longer in effect and they were allowed to pick up their weapons and fight. When the South lost the War and the Confederate armies gave their parole they promised never to bear weapons against the Union again.

Parrott gun: A rifled artillery piece with a reinforcing band at the rear, or breech. Parrott guns were used by both the Army and the Navy, and ranged from 10-pounders to 300-pounders. They were named after their designer, Robert Parker Parrott.

"Peculiar Institution": Another term for slavery in the South.

Percussion Arm: A musket or rifle-musket that requires a cap to fire. A tiny cap is placed on the gun so that when a trigger is pulled, the hammer strikes the cap. The chemical in the cap (fulminate of mercury) ignites and flame shoots into the chamber that holds the gunpowder. This ignites the powder and the blast shoots the bullet out of the barrel. (Percussion means striking—a drum is a percussion instrument and a gun that uses a hammer to strike a cap is a percussion arm.)

Picket: Soldiers posted on guard ahead of a main force. Pickets included about 40 or 50 men each. Several pickets would form a rough line in front of the main army's camp. In case of enemy attack, the pickets usually would have time to warn the rest of the force.

Pontoon Bridge: (pronounced pawn-TOON) A floating bridge which was constructed by anchoring a series of large, flat-bottomed boats across a waterway and then laying wooden planks across them. The planks (the "chess") were anchored by side rails and then covered with a layer of soil to protect it and to dampen sounds. Pontoon bridges were extremely important to the outcome of several battles, including Fredericksburg.

Popular Sovereignty: (pronounced *sov-rin-tee*) This doctrine was prominent during the debate over slavery in the territories. Popular sovereignty said that the people of each territory should be able to decide for themselves if slavery should be allowed in their territory when it became a state.

"Powder Monkey": A sailor (sometimes a child) who carried explosives from the ship's magazine to the ship's guns.

Private: The lowest rank in the army.

"Quaker Guns": Large logs painted to look like cannons; used to fool the enemy into thinking a position was stronger than it really was.

Quartermaster: The officer who was responsible for supplying clothing, supplies and food for the troops.

Rampart: A large earthen mound used to shield the inside of a fortified position from artillery fire and infantry assault. Occasionally ramparts might be constructed of other materials, such as sandbags.

Ramrod: Long, cylindrical metal rod used to push the cartridge down the barrel of a musket in preparation for firing.

Ratify: To formally approve or sanction. **Rebel Yell**: A high-pitched cry that Confederate soldiers would shout when attacking. First heard at First Manassas (First Bull Run) Union troops found the eerie noise unnerving.

Rebel: Loyal to the Confederate States. Also Southern or Confederate.

Reconstruction: A term used to describe the time in American history directly after the Civil War during which the South was "reconstructed" by the North after its loss in the war.

Recruits: The term used to describe new soldiers.

Redan: (pronounced *ri-dan*) A fortification with two parapets or low walls whose faces unite to form a salient angle towards the enemy. That is, they form a point that juts out past the rest of the defensive line of works.

Redoubt: (pronounced *rih-dowt*) An enclosed field work - without redans - which had several sides and was used to protect a garrison from attacks from several directions. While redoubts could be very useful, one key weakness was that each protruding angle was a salient. This meant that the redoubt would be susceptible to enfilading fire. A redoubt could also extend from a permanent fortress.

Reenforcements: Troops sent to strengthen a fighting force by adding an additional number of fresh soldiers.

Regiment: The basic unit of the Civil War soldiers, usually made up of 1,000 to 1,500 men. Regiments were usually designated by state and number (as in 20th Maine). 1 company = 50 to 100 men, 10 companies = 1 regiment, about 4 regiments = 1 brigade, 2 to 5 brigades = 1 division, 2 or more divisions = 1 corps, 1 or more corps = 1 army.

Republican Party: A political party created in the 1850s to prevent the spread of slavery to the territories. Eventually Republicans came to oppose the entire existence of slavery. Abraham Lincoln was the first Republican president. Very few Southerners were Republicans.

Reserve(s): Part(s) of the army which were withheld from fighting during a particular battle but ready and available to fight if necessary.

Revetment: A structure built to hold either natural or man-made embankments in position. Revetments could be made of items such as sandbags, fascines, gabions, brick, stone, and so on. See image »

Revolver: A handheld firearm with a chamber to hold multiple bullets (usually 6). The chamber turns so that each bullet can be fired in succession without reloading.

Revenue Cutter: This term applies to fast ships that were used to patrol the seas and Great Lakes to prevent smuggling and impose importation and custom fees. Revenue cutters would go on to become the United States Coast Guard.

Rifle-Musket: The common weapon of the Civil War infantryman, it was a firearm fired from the shoulder. It differed from a regular musket by the grooves (called rifling) cut into the inside of the barrel. When the exploding powder thrusts the bullet forward, the grooves in the barrel make it spin, just like a football spirals through the air. Rifle-muskets were more accurate and had a longer range than smoothbore weapons.

Rifle Pit: Similar to what soldiers call a "foxhole" today. Rifle pits were trenches with earth mounded up at the end as protection from enemy fire. A soldier lay in the trench and fired from a prone position.

Rifled: A gun barrel is rifled when it has grooves (called rifling) cut into the inside of the barrel for longer range and more accurate firing.

Rout: A crushing defeat where, often, the losers run from the field.

Salient: (pronounced *SAY-lee-uhnt*) A part of a defensive line of works or a fortification that juts out from the main line towards the enemy. Salients can be very vulnerable to because they may be attacked from multiple sides.

Salt Pork: Salt pork is a pork product similar to bacon that is made by curing pork bellies in salt. This curing process aloud the pork to last a very long time without the need for refrigeration. As a result, salt pork became a common food issued to soldiers by both the North and the South.

Sap Roller: A very large, bullet resistant gabion which was used to protect soldiers from enemy fire as they constructed trenches. **Scurvy:** (pronounced *SKUR-vee*) A disease caused by lack of ascorbic acid (found in fresh fruits and vegetables). Its symptoms include spongy gums, loose teeth, and bleeding into the skin and mucous membranes.

Secession: (pronounced *si-sesh-uhn*) Withdrawal from the Federal government of the United States. Southern states, feeling persecuted by the North, seceded by voting to separate from the Union. Southerners felt this was perfectly legal but Unionists saw it as rebellion.

Sectionalism: Promoting the interests of a section or region (such as the North or the South) instead of the entire country.

Sentry: (pronounced *SEHN-tree*) A soldier standing guard.

Shebangs: (pronounced *sheh-bang*) The crude shelters Civil War prisoners of war built to protect themselves from the sun and rain.

Shoddy: Term for cheap, poorly made cloth which was used early in the war to make Federal uniforms. The cloth fell apart very quickly. Eventually "shoddy" became a term for inferior, poorly made items.

Shot: A solid, round projectile, shot from a cannon.

Shell: A hollow projectile, shot from a cannon; a shell was filled with powder and lit by a fuse when it was fired. Shells exploded when their fuse burned down to the level of the powder. Depending on the length of the fuse, artillerymen could decide when they wanted the shell to burst.

Siege: (pronounced *seej*) Blocking the supply lines and escape routes of a city to force it to surrender. A siege usually meant one army trapped in a city, slowly running out of food and fresh water, with the opposing army camped outside. Famous sieges were held at Petersburg, Vicksburg, and Port Hudson.

Siegelines: Lines of works and fortifications that are built by both armies during a siege. The defenders build earthworks to strengthen their position inside a fort or city against assault while the besieging army constructs fortifications to protect siege guns and soldiers from sharpshooters inside the city.

Skirmish: A minor fight.

Slavery: A state of bondage in which African Americans (and some Native Americans) were owned by other people, usually white, and forced to labor on their behalf.

Smoothbore: A gun is smoothbore if the inside of the barrel is completely smooth. Smoothbore guns were used before rifled guns were developed. Although smoothbores were not as accurate and had a shorter range than rifled arms, there were still plenty of them in use during the Civil War.

Sortie: A type of counter-attack used to disrupt the enemy's attack or siege of a fortification, causing the enemy to divert some of its resources away from the initial attack or siege.

South: Also called the Confederacy, the Confederate States of America, or (by Northerners) the Rebel states, the South incorporated the states that seceded from the United States of America to form their own nation. Southern states were: Alabama, Arkansas, Florida, Georgia, Louisiana, Mississippi, North Carolina, South Carolina, Tennessee, Texas, and Virginia.

Spike: To make an artillery piece unusable so that it could not be used by the enemy if captured.

Standard: A flag or banner carried into battle on a pole.

States Rights: This doctrine held the powers of the individual states as greater than the powers of the Federal government. States rights meant that the Federal government held its power only through the consent of the states and that any powers not specifically given to the Federal government remained in control of the states. See the

Stockade: A line of tall stout posts securely set either as a defense, to keep the enemy out, or as a pen to keep prisoners in.

Surrender: To admit defeat and give up in the face of overwhelming odds. Most defeated generals were able to negotiate surrender terms. These might include items like parole instead of prison for the soldiers or letting officers keep their sidearms.

Territory: Land within the mainland boundaries of the country that had not yet become a state by 1861. Nevada Territory, Utah Territory, and Colorado Territory had basically the same boundaries they have today as states; Washington Territory encompassed today's states of Washington and Idaho; Dakota Territory is now the states of Montana, North Dakota, South Dakota, and the northern part of Wyoming; Nebraska Territory today is the southern part of Wyoming and the state of Nebraska; New Mexico Territory included the states of Arizona and New Mexico; and the remaining unorganized land, also called the Indian Territory, filled the approximate boundaries of Oklahoma.

Theater: A theater of war is a region or area where fighting takes place.

Torpedoes: Today called mines, Civil War torpedoes were mostly used by the Confederates. Sometimes they were buried in the ground in the enemy's path to explode when stepped on. Mostly they were used as water defenses. They floated below the surface of the water and exploded when the hull of a ship brushed against them.

Torpedo Boats: Small submersible vessels with long wooden spars mounted on the bow for ramming enemy ships. Torpedoes were lashed to the tip of the spar to explode on impact.

Total War: A new way of conducting war appeared during the Civil War. Instead of focusing only on military targets, armies conducting total war destroyed homes and crops to demoralize and undermine the civilian base of the enemy's war effort. (Sherman in Georgia or Sheridan in the Shenandoah Valley, for example.)

Traverse: A mound of earth used to protect gun positions from explosion or to defilade the inside of a field work or fortification.

Typhoid: Bacterial disease causing fever, diarrhea, headache, enlargement of the spleen, and extreme physical exhaustion and collapse.

Union: Also called the North or the United States, the Union was the portion of the country that remained loyal to the Federal government during the Civil War. Union states were: Connecticut, Delaware, Illinois, Indiana, Iowa, Kansas, Maine, Massachusetts, Michigan, Minnesota, New Hampshire, New Jersey, New York, Ohio, Pennsylvania, Rhode Island, Vermont, and Wisconsin. West Virginia became a Northern state in 1863 and California and Oregon were also officially Northern but they had little direct involvement in the War.

U.S. Christian Commission: An organization established in 1861 for the relief of Union soldiers; the Christian Commission provided food, Bibles, and free writing materials to the soldiers to encourage them in good moral behavior.

U.S.C.T.: United States Colored Troops. Federal Army regiments composed of African-American soldiers. The U.S.C.T.'s were **established by General Order Number 143**, issued May 22, 1863, and included infantry, cavalry and artillery regiments. While the soldiers themselves were African American, officers were white. Until 1864 African American soldiers received less pay than their white counterparts. The most famous USCT regiment is the 54th Massachusetts, composed of free Northern men. The 33rd USCT regiment, however, has the distinction of being the first federally authorized regiment. Composed of freed slaves, it was originally called the 1st South Carolina Volunteer Infantry.

U.S. Sanitary Commission: A government agency created on June 18, 1861, whose purpose was to coordinate female volunteers who were supporting the Federal army. These women collected over $25 million in donations from "Sanitary Fairs" and other fundraisers. The volunteers also made uniforms and bandages, worked as cooks, and nursed the sick and wounded. Leadership, however, was largely male.

Vedette (or vidette): A mounted sentry stationed in advance of a picket line.

Volunteer: Someone who does something because they want to, not because they need to. Most Civil War soldiers, especially in the beginning of the War, were volunteers. Men joined the armies on both sides because they wanted to fight for their cause.

West Point: The United States Military Academy at West Point, New York was the military school for more than 1,000 officers in both the Union and Confederate armies—including Robert E. Lee and Ulysses S. Grant.

Whig Party: A political party generally against slavery and its expansion into the territories. The Whig party had basically been swallowed up by the Democrat and Republican parties by the time of the Civil War.

Works: Fortified structures designed to strengthen a position in battle. This includes earthworks, fieldworks, entrenchments, siege lines, etc.

Yankee: A Northerner; someone loyal to the Federal government of the United States. Also, Union, Federal, or Northern.

Zouave: (pronounced *zoo-ahv* or *zwahv*) A zouave regiment was characterized by its soldiers' bright, colorful uniforms which usually included baggy trousers, a vest, and a fez in different combinations of red, white, and blue. American zouave units were found in both Union and Confederate armies. They were modeled after French African troops who were known for their bravery and marksmanship.

Letters Home

The letters sent home by Frank and John Rieley during their service in the Civil War of the United States of America.

Monroeville, O.
September 5, 1861

Dear Mother:

When I left home, I had no thought of coming to this place, but it was my intention to go to Columbus, Ohio, and enlist there. I had started on foot and got as far as Shelby, Ohio, a distance of sixty seven miles from Cleveland, yesterday, and feeling pretty tired, had stopped there for a rest, which I fell in with a man who was recruiting for a Cavalry Company, and I made up my mind to go with it, and started for this place the same night. We shall probably stay at this place five or six weeks. We are quartered in two or three houses and well fed with pork, beans, potatoes, beef, bread and butter and plenty of coffee. I am well satisfied.

You may well wonder that I should leave a situation where I could make an easy living and enlist as a soldier, but believe that I did not want to do it because I hated work, but I did it because it was my duty to do it, and I think it is the duty of at least one out of each family to go and fight for his country. Because some, that we think should do so, do not, is no excuse for us and Mother I never shall have it said that there was none of a large family of us to go. I never could lift up my head among the citizens of my native land if I had not. You may saw that I owe my parents more than I owe the Country, but I consider that I am doing a duty that they will some day be thankful for. If I get safely through with this war as I hope I shall, it will help me along a little and people will know that I have grit in me.

I wish my brother, John, would go to the book store and get me the cavalry tactics and send them to me and I will pay him.

Write soon and direct your letters to Monroeville, Ohio.

I would have said more if I could. Give my love to all the family.

F. Rieley
Monroeville, O.

Monroeville[1],
September 27, 1861

Dear Mother:

I received your letter of the 23rd this morning and was very glad to hear from home. I would have answered yours of the 9th if I had not thought there would be some changes in the regiment before this time. The regiment to which I belong was raised by Colonel Zahm,[2] and is at present quartered in the town and quartered in four or five old houses but we expect to get into camp this week or next and expect to get our uniforms in about two weeks and our horses and equipment in two months. The Company to which I belong was raised in and around Shelby[2]. Our officers are not elected yet, but we will elect them Monday or Tuesday and I will let you know in my next letter.

Dear mother, I am afraid I have hurt you by leaving home, but you must not feel bad on my account, as I will never do anything of which you or any of the family would be ashamed, and Mother, do not fret yourself about me. I cannot find room to answer all your questions, but I think I can get a furlough in three or four weeks and I will tell you all about my adventures. Tell Pa not to feel uneasy about me as I have a strong constitution and am able to stand hardships. I have seen no one since I left home that I know, but have not felt lonesome because of the novelty of the situation. I have gotten the books which you wrote about. I would like to have you sent the Cleveland Plain Dealer[3] once and a while. I like camp life so far, but it will be hard when Winter sets in.

The regiment will not leave this place for months yet. I would have answered that first letter, but I was waiting until we got into camp which I though we would do before now. We drill once a day on foot. This regiment is the 4th regiment of cavalry.

Give my love to all the family. I remain your affectionate son.

Frank

---

[1] A village in Huron County, Ohio

[2] Shelby is located in Richland County, Ohio, on the Mohican River

[3] Newspaper was established in 1842, less than 50 years after Moses Cleaveland landed on the banks of the Cuyahoga River in Ohio

Monroeville, O.

Camp Worcester[4],

October 19, 1861

Dear Mother and Friends:

I take this opportunity to write you a few lines. I received your letter of the 9th a few days ago, but could not find a chance to write before.

Our time is nearly all taken up in drilling and have very little time to spare. We have received our caps, shirts, drawers and boots, and expect to receive the rest of our uniforms next week. The Company to which I belong is Company I, 3rd Ohio Cavalry. The officers of the Company are: Captain – H.B. Gaylord, 1st Lieutenant – Clark Center, 2nd Lieutenant – Wm, Goodnon. The Captain has appointed me 2nd Corporal. The regiment is nearly full and we have part of our horses and will have all of them in a week or two. The Officers of the regiment are Colonel – Lewis Zahm, Lieutenant Colonel – D.A. Maury. We have three Majors – one of them is Major Foster. The adjutant is the Colonel's son. There is some talk of the regiment being sent to Camp Dennison[5] in about two weeks.

I am sorry to hear that brother John wants to enlist. If I had thought he wanted to enlist, I would have staid at home. This camp is about a mile and a half from town and is well situated and covers three or four acres of land. We have a creek running near it which empties into the Huron River. The town is about fifteen miles south of Sandusky, Ohio and on the line of the Cleveland Toledo Road.

I have never felt better in my life than I do now. I have received three papers from home for which I am thankful. I am in want of nothing here but money and I find it hard to get along without it. I am pretty sure of getting a furlough and I think I can go home for ten days. If I can, I will. I shall talk to you about writing to the Plain Dealer when I get home. How does brother Sylvester[6] and the rest of the children get along.

Give my love to all the family and tell John not to enlist until I get home. From your son,

Frank

Direct your letters to Frank Rieley, Company I 3rd Cavalry, Monroeville, Ohio.

---

[4] Camp Worcester, an Army camp at Monroeville, Ohio that was in use from 1861 to 1862

[5] Camp Dennison, a military recruiting, training, and medical post for the United States Army during the American Civil War. It was located near Cincinnati, Ohio, not far from the Ohio River. The camp was named for Cincinnati native William Dennison, Ohio's governor at the start of the war.

[6] Edwin Sylvester Rieley, one of the siblings of Frank and John Rieley

27

Camp Worcester
Monroeville, Ohio
November 13, 1861

Dear Mother:

I received your letter of the 4th soon after date and was very glad to hear from home. I am well and in good spirits.

We have received our uniforms and are well pleased with them. They consist of a dark colored jacket and light blue pants. We have not received all of our overcoats yet, but expect them soon. They are light blue and very warm and good. We have all or our horses and part of our bridles. The regiment lacks about one hundred men of being full.

The dollar that you were so kind as to send me was very acceptable as I was very much in need of some money.

I shall have to close my letter now and go draw our rations.

The Captain has promised me a furlough and I think I shall be home Friday or Saturday.

Yours truly,

Frank Rieley

Camp Worcester,
December 4, 1861

Dear Mother:

You must think that I have been very unkind in not writing before, but I have been sick a week with sore throat and I have not been able to write before. I am now well however and doing first rate.

It is getting pretty cold here and we are all anxious to be moving farther south. We have the tent in which I am, raised up and a stove in it and we are very nearly as comfortable as we would be at home, but we have some in camp who have no stoves and very few blankets. Those must suffer. We have not yet got our saddles and do not know when we will get them.

Company K which is not full have elected their officers today and will be soon full and I think that as soon as it is full, we will move from there. The weather here has been very cold and stormy, snowing most of the time. Today is a pleasant day. It has been three months today since I enlisted and have not received any pay. I expect we will though before we move from here.

I suppose brother John told you that I arrived safely back at camp. Those gloves are first rate this cold weather and I do not know what I should have done without them. I must stop now and hoping that you will write soon.

Frank Rieley

Camp Worcester
December 9, 1861

Dear Mother:

 Was glad to have your last letter. Our regiment was invited by the people of Norwalk[7] to a dinner, speech making etc., at which we were presented with a flag, a cannon etc. after we had received all our horses and saddles. We had a nice time.

Write soon, love to all.

Frank Rieley

---

[7] Norwalk, a city in Huron County, Ohio, United States. Norwalk is located approximately 10 miles (16 km) south of Lake Erie, 51 miles (82 km) west/southwest of Cleveland, 59 miles (95 km) southeast of Toledo, and 87 miles (140 km) north/northeast of Columbus

Camp Worcester
December 29, 1861

Dear Mother:

I received your letter of the 24th soon after date and was very glad to hear from home.

We have fine weather here for this time of year. We have not received marching orders but we have orders to hold ourselves ready to march at an hours notice and I think it probable that we will move next week. We have not received any pay and do not know when we will get any. I spent Christmas better than I thought I would. David Taylor is a Corporal in Company M of this regiment and his wife has been in Monroeville for about a week past. She was at Wm. Sinclair's house the day before Christmas and he sent up word by here to have me come down and dine with them on Xmas. I in company with Dave and his wife went down and had a first rate dinner. Our Captain presented each mess a fine turkey for Christmas. Col. Zahm's affairs are all settled. I should like to go home again but no more furloughs are allowed. You said in your letter that if I didn't have money for postage to sent it as I did the one right after I was sick. I paid the adjutant for the postage and every other letter that I have sent since being here so that they adjutant must have put the postage in his own pocket.

Give my love to all the family,

Francis Rieley

January 20th, 1962
Camp at Monroeville, O.

Dear Mother:

I received your last letter soon after date and was very glad to hear from home. I should have answered it then but we were too busy getting ready to leave that I could not find time.

The regiment commenced leaving Monroeville on the 13th. The last two companies left on the 18th. Company I left here by horse back to Shelby, Ohio on the 15th from there by train to Camp Dennison. A ball was given Company I at Shelby and we had a first rate time. On the road from Monroeville to Shelby we were furnished all the pies, cakes, apples, etc. we could eat and carry. The Company did not stay in Columbus any longer than to change engines, reaching Camp Dennison on the 17th which was a camp of three hundred acres. The camp consisted of about eight thousand men. It is hilly and we could see into Kentucky on clear days. We live in a house one hundred feet long, thirty feet wide and ten feet high and one hundred bunks. Another house was the kitchen. The quarters are well ventilated and warmed by two large stoves. Sheds for the horses are near the little Miami river where the horses are watered. The camp is very muddy. The 2nd Ohio Cavalry occupied these quarters previous to us and left on the 15th for Kansas.

I shall have to stop writing now, so goodbye until my next.

From your son

Frank

February 2nd, 1862
Camp Dennison, Ohio

Dear Mother:

I received your letter of the 29th yesterday and was very glad to hear from home. I also received the papers of which you spoke in your letter. Things go on about as usual here in camp. Since my last letter, we have received our sabres with which we were well pleased. We have not received any of our other arms yet, but expect them soon.

Camp Dennison is not so disagreeable as you have been told. It is pretty muddy at present but we must expect that at this time of year. The soil is sandy and if we had a few fine days, the mud would dry up in no time. The climate is warmer than up in Cleveland. It hardly freezes at night and when it does freeze, thaws out the next day. We have had only one snow storm since I have been here and that went the next day.

I have been promoted to 1st Corporal since I last wrote you, one of our sergeants having received another position in the regiment, and the 1st Corporal was promoted to a sergeant. We expect our pay next week and I fi do get our pay, I expect to get four months pay. When I get my pay, I shall send it home by express to Hugh Rieley, care of J.B. Smith Malster, Cleveland, Ohio. If this does not suit you, write and let me know as soon as you receive this letter. Write anyhow so that I will be sure.

Three cent Postage stamps do not cost six cents apiece here as reported by our friend, Al Bishop.

I will have my likeness taken and send it home as you requested me to as soon as we get the rest of our arms. I have not seen anybody with whom I have been acquainted in Cleveland.

If you hear of anyone being here whom I am acquainted let me know as there are so many men here, it is impossible to find anyone unless you know where to look for them. I am thankful for the papers you sent me. I have no money to buy papers or anything else.

Love to all the family. Yours etc.

Frank.

Camp Wright
February 23, 1862
Jeffersonville, Ind.

Dear Mother:

It is a very long time since I have heard from home, and I suppose the reason that I have received no letters from home is because you have been waiting for a letter from me.

The reason I have not written before is partly because I have had no money nor paper to write with and partly because I was waiting for a letter from home.

We left Camp Dennison on the 10th and reached this place the next day. We were ordered here in somewhat of a hurry. The Colonel having received a dispatch to leave only the day before we left. We left Camp Dennison in the morning and went to Cincinnati on horseback, and from there we came down on a steamboat.

We didn't have much chance to see Cincinnati when we came through, only a few of the streets. We left there about 11:00 P.M. It was very dark and the boat had to stop in the night, until it got lighter. We reached here without any accident the next morning about 10 o'clock.

Jeffersonville is right opposite Louisville, Kentucky, about five thousand inhabitants. We were told when we left Camp Dennison that we were going to Louisville, but when we got there we were taken to the Indiana shore. How long we will stay here I do not know.

When I last wrote you we all expected to get our pay very soon after, but we were all fooled about it. Although our Officers tell us we will get it next week, we do not believe them. They have been telling that ever since we left Camp Worcester. I am very hard up for money as all the regiment are. I had hard work to borrow the paper on which I am writing. The Captain Bartlett battery of artillery from Cleveland are encamped with us here and I thin that when we go, they will go with us. Tom Burrows is in that battery, also Mr. Sliney's son of whom you spoke in your last letter. I received the letter from Mr. Sliney directing where to send the money.

Write as soon as you received this. Love to all the family.

Frank Rieley

Bowling Green, Ky.
March 14, 1862

Dear Mother:

I received your letter of the 5th yesterday and was very glad to hear from you.

We left Jeffersonville the 2nd with orders to march to this place and reached here yesterday. First we crossed the river to Louisville and marched four miles in the rain. That night we camped in the mud and water and the next morning we started again with our clothes all wet and it having commenced freezing, they were soon all frozen. We marched all this day. The next day we had a fine day to march. We stopped one day at Bardstown and one day at Mumfordville. Bardstown has about ten thousand inhabitants. Mumfordville has about five thousand. At the last place the railroad bridge was blown up by the rebels and across the river (Green River) is where the first fighting was one in Kentucky. The bridge was repaired by Union men and we crossed the river on it. It is about 170 feet high and 15' wide, and it makes a person almost shudder to look down to the water. There are large breast works on the south side of the river, which were built by our men. The fight was about a mile south of the town and it was here that four hundred of our men cleaned out twenty five hundred of the enemy. On our road from Munfordville to this place, we camped near Mammoth Cave[8] of which we have heard so much, and at night I visited the cave. I have not time to give you an account of the cave now, but I will some time, when I have time.

Bowling Green is quite a City of about twenty thousand, about one quarter of the houses are empty, having been left by the Secessionists, when our troops came. There are large fortifications on the hills around to town which were left by the rebels. Both the railroad and turnpike bridge were burned at this place. We start in the morning for Nashville.

I have not had time to have a likeness taken or I would. You say you have not had any letter from me when you got the money. I wrote one and put it in the package with the money. I have received only one paper since we left Camp Dennison.

Love to all the folks,

Frank Rieley

---

[8] A cave system in Kentucky with over 390 miles (630 km) of passageways

Camp Jackson near Nashville
March 28, 1862

Dear Mother and Sister:

I received your letter of the 24th today and was very glad to hear from home. The reason that you was so long in hearing from me, was that we had been on the march for two weeks, and I was unable to find time to write and I did not receive your letter until we got to Bowling Green. If you could see how eagerly I read the letters from home, you would think I was as anxious to hear from you as you. The mail is very irregular but I will write every chance I get and let you know how I get along. I have only received five or six papers since I left Camp Dennison.

The money I sent is the same as I received it. We were paid for a little over three months to January 1st.

That was a good letter of yours and I hope you will send one like it every time you write. I like to hear how the folks get along at home. We have at last had a chance to rest ourselves and horses after the long march that we had. We were on the road nineteen days.

We are now camped about four miles south of Nashville. We have been here eight days. The 41st Ohio left here the day before we came here. I was sorry not to have seen Dick Neville of the 41st. They went somewhere south of here. There are a lot of Secesh[9] around here but they do not molest us. Nashville is a city of about sixty thousand most Secesh. They do not say anything as the city is well guarded by our men. A guard to almost every house. One of our soldiers was shot in the City by a seceshionist the other night, but the Secesh was caught the next day and was court marshalled and hanged by our men. Our regiment is in General Woods division, so when you see in the papers about Gen. Woods division moving, you will know where I am. We have received orders to move in the morning at 3 o'clock, further south. When we stop again, I will write.

The weather is pleasant and warm as it is at home in May. The negroes here are plowing their masters fields. I have seen no white men working since I came into Tennessee. The peach trees are in blossom and there is every indication of Spring.

I am well except for a slight cold. There are a great many men sick in the regiment at present mostly from diarrhea. I shall have to stop writing as it is dark. Write soon and direct as before.

Love to all the family.

---

[9] A slang abbreviation for a secessionist, citizens of the eleven Southern states that declared their secession for the United States and formed the Confederate States of American in 1861. Known during the Civil War as 'rebels.'

I got the postage stamps.

Frank Rieley

April 13, 1862
Camp near Savannah, Tenn.

(Shiloh)

Dear Mother:

I promised to write as soon as I stopped and am now fulfilling the promise. We left Nashville March 29ᵗʰ at the head of Woods Division twelve thousand men including the artillery, infantry and cavalry. We passed through several small towns, the largest was Franklin. Columbia, was of a good size. The fourth day of our march, eight companies of our regiment were sent to the main road to a small town called Lawrenceburg. It was reported that five hundred Secesh were there. We started early in the morning and reached our objection at 2 P.M. and went dashing through the town with our sabres drawn all ready for a fight, but the Secesh had flown just a half hour before. Our Lt. Colonel started us in pursuit. Co I and G to ok the road leading south, the rest of the regiment took other roads. The road we were on was the right one, as we had proceeded seven miles we caught site of them, they started to run. Their horses being fresh, they were able to get away from us.

We again got under way to this place. Sunday the 7ᵗʰ, we heard heavy firing in this direction and a messenger came with a message for us to hurry up and said there was a hard battle going on near Pittsburg which is about four miles from Savannah. He said also that our men were getting the worst of it. We hurried as fast as possible and got to this place the next day. When we were ordered to stay, as there was more cavalry at the battle than they could use, so we were not in the big fight.

You must have heard all about it before you get this and have a better account of it in the papers than I could give you. The most pitiable sight I ever saw was seeing the wounded brought in, some with a leg shot off or an arm, some with a shot in the head. One poor man had one of his eyes shot out. The wounded came in as fast as two boats could bring them across the river for five days.

I shall write you again in a few days and send me a few postage stamps as they are ten cents apiece here.

Love to all the family.

Frank Rieley

Pittsburg Landing, Tenn.
Camp Shiloh[10]
May 7, 1862

Dear Mother:

Received your letter of the 8th a week after date and was very glad to hear
from home and also to hear you were all well. The reason I did not answer it
then was that I expected we would cross the Tennessee River and I did not
want to write until after we crossed it. We are on the other side of the river
for about three weeks, scouting and guarding a telegraph line. We crossed to
this side on the 25th to Pittsburg Landing. It is composed of two log houses
one of which is the postoffice.

We camped on the battle field of Shiloh the first night. The next day we
moved about three miles and rejoined our division. We could not see much
signs of the battle except on the trees which were full of bullet holes, and
some of them cut in two by cannon balls. The graves were very thick. I saw
one hole where there were twenty of our boys buried. The men who were in
the battle told me some holes had fifty buried in them. Our men did not half
bury the Secesh soldiers. I saw where one was buried whose hands stuck out.
I went over to the 41st Ohio last week and saw Dick Neville. He was in the
fight but was not hurt. He feels first rate and is ready for the next fight.
Michael Miller was wounded in the arm. He started for home soon after the
fight, so I suppose you have seen him before this. We moved to our camp
here on the 29th. We camped about six miles from Pittsburg Landing and
about twelve from Corinth, and two miles from the Mississippi line. I was on
the picket line night before last and was in Mississippi.

There is a report in camp today that Corinth is being evacuated, but we do not
know for sure. If it is, we will have to follow them three or four hundred
miles further I suppose. I should a good deal rather fight them here than
follow them three hundred miles further, and then have to fight them. I think
that the next time they are whipped, it will finish them.

I am well and in good spirits. We were paid off today for two months and I
will send twenty five dollars home with this letter. Our Chaplain is going
home on furlough and I will send it with him to Monroeville and he will send
it by express to the same directions as before. If you get this and the money,
write and let me know.

Give my love to all.

Frank Rieley

---

[10] A camp near the location of the Battle of Shiloh, located in south central Tennessee, which marked a turning point in
the Civil War.

May 21ˢᵗ, 1862

Camp in Woods – 5 miles

from Corinth,¹¹ Miss.

Dear Mother:

I received your letter of the 20ᵗʰ of April and also yours of the 15ᵗʰ, I received yesterday. I was very glad to hear from home and also to hear that you were all well. I should have answered your first letter before this, but I was waiting for the battle to come off which I expected before this.

I am well and in good shape and spirits and spoiling for a fight. There has been no general engagement here as yet although we expect it every day. There are scrimmages every day between our pickets and the rebels in which our men generally come off best. Our army is throwing up breast works about two miles from Corinth. I think as soon as our men get these finished the fight will come off. Probably before this reaches you, Corinth will be ours. I don't think there will be as large a battle as some suppose because every deserter from the rebel army is greatly demoralized, not having enough to eat and no clothing to wear.

Our soldiers here are delighted with the victory in the east and want to whip the rebels here and get home and I think if we give them a sound thrashing here, we will be home very soon.

I think we have them pretty well surrounded here and if we whip them, we will take their whole army and this will wind up the Confederacy. If they whip us, we will have our breast works to fall back on, but let us hope that we will not have to fall back. General Nelson's Division is on the left of General Wood's division and I will have a chance to see Dick Neville once in a while, as I saw him a week ago in Nelson' Division.

As soon as the battle is over, I will write you again.

F. Rieley

---

¹¹ Located in northern Mississippi, Corinth was a primary gateway to the battlefield at Shiloh and a strategic objective of both the Union and Confederate Armies being at the intersection of two rail lines.

Corinth, Miss.
June 9ʰ, 1862

Dear Mother:

You have no doubt heard long before this of the evacuation of this place by the rebels. Our regiment was among the first in there after the rebels had left. We chased them three or four miles but being without rations, we had to return to town and sent out scouting parties and they brought in a great many prisoners. The town looks very hard. The inhabitants had all left and a great many houses were in ashes and others burning. There were large quantities of salt pork and beef, beans and sugar and other commissary stores burned up before they left, also wagons, tents, and cotton. The rebels have outwitted our generals that is sure. They got everything away they could and burned the rest. Those things that could not be carried, they cutup with axes. Especially the water buckets. There were none left in the whole town.

They were very far from starving to death as reported. Their camps were almost covered with biscuits and salt pork and beef, having plenty of everything except coffee and salt.

The live on biscuits while we live on hard crackers. Deserters from the rebels say they had only about fifty thousand men fit for duty in Corinth and about as many men sick. We could have taken them all or nearly all if our generals had attacked them before the commenced leaving, but perhaps it is better as it is.

On the 5ʰ, our battalion (the 3ʳᵈ) was ordered to pack up and report to General Nelson[12]. We got ready and marched to his headquarters and the whole division took up their march to some place unknown. We took the road leading south from Corinth, passed through a small town called Danville, and camped about ten miles south of Corinth. The next day rested but two days following, we marched ten miles more. Part of our Company was ordered back to Pittsburg Landing for rations, I went along.

Nelson's division was ordered to move on about the 20ʰ. I sent a letter home since then, did you receive it? Write soon, yours, etc.

Francis Rieley

---

[12] A Major General in the Union Army who led the 4ᵗʰ Division of the Army of Ohio, killed in August 1862 over an insult by another Union General.

June 20, 1862
Tuscumbia, Ala.

Dear Mother:

We took all our baggage and started to this place. On our road, we passed through the town of Iuka 1500 inhabitants, where we left Nelson's division and came to this place where we joined our regiment, which was still with Wood's division.

We came through a better country than any we saw around Corinth or any since Nashville.

The soil is sandy and rolling countryside make it pleasing. Plenty of good water and several large plantations with 140 to 150 negroes working. They raise mostly corn, but I saw a cotton field with 200 acres.

We are encamped on the west side of Tuscumbia which is a fine town, two miles from the Tennessee River. A find Spring. A few days ago, we were ordered to turn in our overcoats, jackets and all spare baggage, half our tents and part of wagons to division headquarters. We think we are about to start on a long march.

Am sending home some confederate postage stamps.

Love,

Frank

July 8ᵗʰ, 1862
Decatur, Ala.

Dear Mother:

In my last letter, I told you we turned in our baggage and expected to move from Tuscumbia.

We did not move for some time after I wrote. On the 21ˢᵗ of June, Co. I and C were aroused at 7 P.M. and ordered to go to the town of Russellville, twenty miles south. We expected some rebels there but found none. We stayed there a week and had a great many deserters came in. Eight Union men came in a joined our regiment. We kept a sharp lookout for two companies of rebels reported near. We were relieved by two companies of our own regiment and ordered back to Tuscumbia. One day of rest there and we moved on to Decatur, Alabama.

We went through good country. We then crossed, in a day or so, the Tennessee River on a Tennessee gunboat which was pretty small, to the M & C R. R.[13] about eight miles north.

Love,

Frank

---

[13] The Memphis and Charleston (M&C) Railroad was a link in a chain of early railroads connecting the Atlantic Coast to the Mississippi River.

Woodsville, Ala.
August 1862

Dear Mother:

Soon after the last letter was written we were ordered to Woodsville from Decatur, July 9th, under the command of Lt. Col. Murray, and marched fourteen miles through good farming country.

The next morning we proceeded to Huntsville. It is a fine town, best I have seen in the South. There is a large locomotive works here and two good carriage shops.

We then proceeded to Woodsville. The country is mountainous and scenery is fine. Most of the town as burned by Gen. Mitchell because one of his trains was fired up and run off the track by bush whackers.[14] We were sent here to clean them out. They had given our men a great deal of trouble on the railroad. We have them cleaned out pretty well. A few days ago our battalion and a regiment of infantry and two cannons went to the river to destroy a ferry boat which the rebels used to cross the river with. We started from here on the 27th and got there the next morning. There was a town on the other side of the river (The Tennessee) called Guntersville. Our cannon opened on the town with shells. The rebels shot from behind trees and wounded a couple of our men. We destroyed the ferry boat and a lot of stores and boats at two other landings. Two regiments were ahead of us on the return to Woodsville and a Soldier was killed by a bush whacker. We searched for the bush whacker for an hour or so but could not find him.

Frank

[14] Bushwackers were part of the irregular military forces on both sides during the American Civil War. Fighting in a form of guerilla warfare, bushwackers attacked whomever they thought were legitimate targets, usually in rural areas.

October 5, 1862
Shepherdsville, Ky.

Dear Mother:

It is now a long time since I wrote you and you must have been very anxious to know where I am. I should have written before this if we had not been out of communication with the North and this is the first chance I have had to send a letter home for six weeks.

We left Woodsville, Ala. September 20th and leaving four companies and all our baggage there, and went on cars via M & C R. R. to Stevenson, and from there took cars on the Nashville and Chattanooga Railroad to a place called Deckard, eighty miles south of Nashville, where we got a lot of new horses. We laid there until the rest of the regiment came up. On the way over the mountains, they lost the tents and baggage belonging to our company. I lost my shirts and some other things I had left behind. From Deckard, we went to Shelbyville and from there to Murfreesboro[15] where we laid two or three days. We were here put into Cavalry Brigade (3 and 4 Ohio and the 5th Ky. Cavalry) and commanded by Col. Zahn. From Murfreesboro to Nashville, we were rear guard for the whole of Buell's army. The rebels were right behind us and I stood picket duty right in sight of the rebel pickets but we did not have any trouble with them. From Nashville we went to Bowling Green, Ky., where we laid a day and then went on a scout near a place named Glasgow. After we were out a while, the Colonel sent the 3[d] Battalion of the 3[d] on a different road from what the rest took. After following this road for three or four miles, we came upon some rebel pickets and Co. I dismounted and captured them. It was too late however, to attack their camp which was in Glasgow. We went there the next day, but they had left. We however captured three hundred sick and wounded rebels and about one hundred muskets, and four or five wagon loads of flour. From Glasgow, we went to Mumfordsville and from there to Elizabethtown, where we were ordered to go back to Bowling Green and guard a wagon train into Louisville. We guarded it to the mouth of Salt River where we left it. The mouth of the Salt River is thirty miles from Louisville and on the Ohio River, from there we came to this place, Shepherdsville, which is fifteen miles from Louisville, on the L & N R. R. and fifteen miles from the Ohio River. The rebels have left this place only a few days ago and have taken everything they could lay their hands on.

The 1st battalion of our regiment had a fight at Mumfordville and had twelve men killed and wounded but they routed three regiments of rebels cavalry and killed and wounded seventy of them. We have been on the road for six weeks and have not had time to cook our rations and what as worse we have not had

---

[15] A town in Tennessee, named for Revolutionary War hero Colonel Hardy Murfree, Murfreesboro became the capital of Tennessee from 2828 to 1826. In December 1862, Murfreesboro was the site of the bloodiest battle of the Civil War with over 23,000 casualties.

any to cook. I must close as we are ordered to march where I don't know. You must excuse hand writing as I have to write in a hurry.

Frank

Dear Friends at home

I have received yours of the 16th and was very glad to hear from home and hear that Frank was in good health. You sent me his directions but not the letter of the Company and I have forgotten it and will have to wait until you send it to me. I am well and all the boy are except Adam and Stickney and neither of them very bad. Rease got kicked by a horse the other day and it made a hole in his head two inches long. He is around doing well.

We expect to leave here in a day or two for the south. We don't expect to see any fighting in this state. I think we will be in Tennessee or Alabama this winter. I think I will have a chance of seeing Frank or some of the Brooklyn boys. We are so well drilled that the folks around here think that we are all regulars.

Oct. 20th, '62
I did not have time to fishing writing yesterday but will try to do it today. There was a Brigade of hard looking men came into camp the other day from Cumberland Gap[16] where the rebels starved them out. They stayed there until they had not a bit to eat and then stole out in the night. The rebels drove them into Ohio at Portsmouth. The 9th Ohio Battery that was in Camp Wood in Cleveland was with them. They came over mountains where it took a regiment of men to pull their guns over. There are the hardest looking set of men I ever saw.

We are kept so busy that I could hardly find time to write this letter having to get up four or times before I finished it but I feel better than when we layed in camp at Cleveland. I am called again and must stop. Give my love to all. Direct your letters the same as before.

John

---

[16] A location at the point where the states of Tennessee, Virginia, and Kentucky meet. During the War, control of this location changed many times between the Union and Confederate forces.

Note: From the flow of letters written by Frank Rieley to his mother, and comparing that to the actual letters that had been saved, it does appear that there is a letter missing from his time in or near Frankfort, Kentucky.

Whether this letter was never received, or was simply lost, is not known.

Dear Mother:

I received your nice letter of November 9th yesterday and was glad to hear form home once more, also our letter of October 14th. When I wrote you last from Frankfort, Ky where I had gone after Morgan had taken me prisoner.

You asked for information concerning the fight with Morgan. It happened this way. Major Sidell of our regiment with about ninety men of the 3rd Ohio and one hundred men of the 4th Ohio regiments was ordered to go to Camp Dick Robinson near Lexington and guard a lot of pork left there by the rebels in their hasty retreat. We went there and the Major hearing of a small body of rebels at Lexington, thought he would try and capture them. Se we went to Lexington and were the first Union troops that had entered the City since the rebels held possession of it. We were greeted by applause by the residents, waving flags and shouting for the Ohio boys. We camped about two miles from the city that night and the next morning, we were awakened before daylight, saddled up and had just mounted when the pickets were fired upon and we had scarcely got out on the road when we saw a regiment of infantry deployed as skirmishers only a few rods in front of us. Our Company which was in front fell back and dismounted. As we fell back the enemy commenced cheering, but we soon stopped their yells, by a few shots which made them all lay down on the ground. We then saw another regiment of rebels coming up the road and we fell back. Then we saw another line in the rear of us which at first sight we thought was our own men, but we soon found out that they were rebels, and saw at once we were surrounded. Our arms were taken from us and when some of our men had laid down their arms, they fired into them. We were then drawn up in line and while they were paroling some of the men, another boy and myself escaped and went to Frankfort, 200 men, one major and four captains were paroled. We had four men killed and seven men wounded. The enemy had twenty two killed and fifteen wounded. Morgan's force which captured us was 3500 and 9 pieces of artillery.

From Frankfort after Morgan had taken me prisoner and I had escaped as stated above, I went to Louisville on the cars and stopped with some of our regiment who were getting a new supply of horses, our old horses being pretty well run down. We stayed at Louisville about a week and then started for our regiment which was at Lebanon, Ky. Each of us had to lead three or four horses. When we reached Lebanon, the regiment had left there for Mumfordville where we came up with them. The next day we all marched to Bowling Green. We laid there a day. The next day we moved to Gallatin, Tenn. We camped. A part of us were sent on a scout to Gallatin where we found that Morgan had a force of 3500 men too much for us to attack. We then awaited the coming up for Gen. Wood's division, up another road. We had a skirmish in the mountain with the enemy and killed one man and wounded three or four more. The next day after Wood's arrival, we all started for Gallatin. We rushed in but the bird had flown. Morgan had left that night at 12 o'clock. We pursued the rear guard for a few miles, but the enemy had too much start.

We then moved our camp to Gallatin and joined the rest of the Cavalry of the 2nd Co. Division. We then marched to Hartsville. Here our advance had a skirmish with some of Morgan's cavalry killing one and taking several prisoners. We captured 50 mules that the rebels were driving for the rebel army. We encamped on the banks of the Cumberland River for three or four days. The whole division of Cavalry was then ordered to Lebanon, Tenn., reported to have a large force. When we got half way there we were ordered to countermarch for what I don't know. Afterwards heard that Gen. Wood had gone through that place. From Hartsville, we went back to Gallatin and then on to Nashville. On the road, we saw the 41st Ohio with our friends Dick and John Nevel, Charley Chessly, M. Miller. The 1st Battalion are with Woods Division and they had a battle at Mumfordville October 5th.

I am in the 3rd Battalion in the 2nd Cavalry Brigade Col. Zahn. The brigade in the 2nd Division Cavalry, Col. Kennet.

We expect to stay here for sometime and also get pay for eight months, not having been paid since May last.

F. Rieley

Dear Mother and Sister

I received your letter of the 27th and was very glad to hear from home and to hear that all was well. We left Camp Blair Oct. 22nd and arrived at Camp Sutton the 28th which is 90 miles south of Covington and three miles north of Lexington. We stayed there three or four days when we again started for our present camp 2 miles south of Lexington. It is the finest country around here I ever saw – no hills or hollows like the northern part of the state. I am driving a team and have a good chance to see the country. I was in Lexington four times since I have been around here. It is a hard working place.

The name of the Lieutenant is 1st Willson, 1st Duston, 1st Harris, and 2nd Smith. We are in no Division yet – when we are I will let you know. I think we left Covington before Miss Hardman came down – I did not see her. On our march we saw some cold weather – the ground was covered with snow four inches deep part of the time. It soon melted away and it is very pleasant now. I did not hear from Frank yet. The first chance I get I will write to him. The boys are all well. I never felt better. I weighed 73 pounds the other day, the heaviest I ever weighed. I watched at the shanty to see I could see anyone I knew but it was too dark.

Direct your next to Lexington, Ky., instead of Covington. Give my love to all.

John

Dear Mother and Sister

I received your letter of the 9th eight or nine days ago and was very glad to hear from home. I received a letter from Frank the other day which had been on the way over four weeks before I got it. It had the same news in that was in your last letter. I wrote him the next day after I got it. We are in the same place that we were when I last wrote and we expect to stay here for some time, maybe all winter, but I would sooner go farther south. It has been raining here for three days without stopping. The first rain I left home. It is very pleasant today. I have not seen any cold weather yet. Lieutenant Harris fell from a horse the other day and broke his leg just above the ankle. There are quite a number of sick in the Battery. The Burg Boys are all well. I was never better. I have received only three letters from home since I left there. I suppose you have sent more that I have received. I told you in my last letter that you might send me a few postage stamps but if you have not sent them when you received this you need for I have over one dollars worth. Direct the same as before. Write soon. Give my love to all.

John

Dear Mother:

We are still laying where we were when I wrote you last. Since then, we went on a scout to Lebanon, Tenn. which place we heard was occupied by a force of cavalry. They left before we got there.

Lebanon is a pretty good sized town and has a fine college.

From Lebanon we went south about ten miles and camped for the night and started back the next morning for Nashville by another road. After we had went a few miles, we got track of a guerrilla party. We chased them three or four miles and gave up pursuit and returned. We captured a Captain however.

We expect to move to Murfreesboro soon. Gen Rosecrans[17] reviewed our division of cavalry not long ago and told us that he would furnish us with good arms and must take good care of them. The most of the cavalry are armed very poorly at present. I like the appearance of Gen. Rosecrans very well and think he will rush matters when he gets going. We were paid on the 7th for six months. They owe us three months. The green backs were very acceptable, everyone being strapped.

There was an agent of the Governor of Ohio here who was sent to take the money of the soldiers and give them a check on the County Treasury. I thought that was the safest way to sent it, so will enclose the check with this letter and you can go to the Court House in Cleveland and get it. It is for sixty dollars. If you can get it, let me know.

Frank Rieley

---

[17] William Starke Rosecrans (September 6, 1819 – March 11, 1898) gained fame for his role as a Union general during the American Civil War. He was the victor at prominent Western Theater battles, but his military career was effectively ended following his disastrous defeat at the Battle of Chickamauga in 1863.

Louisville, Ky. December 17, 1862

I send with this a few more photos of some of the boys in our company. I sent home a memorial containing the names of all the men who are in Co. I. Have you received it? Everything goes on as usual here and have nothing to write only that it is very muddy, wet and disagreeable at present.

Frank Rieley

Dear Mother and Sister

I received your letter of the 16ᵗʰ today and was very glad to hear from home. We left Lexington over a week since and came to this place. Richmond is 26 miles from Lexington. We came 16 miles the first day and went into a camp on the side of a large hill on the bank of the Kentucky River. We started the next morning at three o'clock and crossed the river on a ferry boat. We arrived safe in Richmond and went into camp where we have stayed since. Richmond is a small town of about 500 inhabitants. The infantry has been throwing up entrenchments ever since we came here and have nearly completed the job. We have about five or six regiments here and expect more everyday. I don't know how long we will stay here but I think it will be for some time. There are no rebel forces this side of Cumberland Gap which is one hundred miles from this place. It is thought they will have to come up this way for provisions soon as there are none on the other side. As I cannot thing of anything more to write I will have to bring this to a close. Give my love to all.

Direct your letters to Richmond, Ky.

John

Camp near Nashville
December 24, 1862

Dear Mother:

Received nice letter on December 18th and was very glad to receive it on the 22nd and know that you are all well.

We do not lay in camp all the time. Our division of cavalry goes on a scout every few days and when not scouting have to do picket duty, guard, forage trains, etc.

Soon after I wrote you the last letter we went on a scout to Franklin, Tenn. When we got about ten miles from Nashville we came upon enemy pickets whom we drove in. We formed line of battle with skirmishers in front of us and drove the rebels for six miles, killing two or three and wounding several. We had six or seven horses killed, no men hurt. We returned six miles and camped for the night. The next day we marched south to Franklin, Tenn. Our regiment was in the rear and did not see the fight. The advance regiment had a man wounded. We captured three wagonloads of flour, two hogshead[18] of sugar and twenty prisoners. Gen. Stanley had command.

We probably will stay at this place until the Cumberland River rises and then move South. Our pickets have skirmishes every day.

I do not think they will attack us here, but wait till we move south.

Merry Xmas and Happy New Year.

Frank

---

[18] A very large wooden barrel that could hold about 1,000 pounds of sugar. A standardized hogshead measured 48 inches (1,219 mm) long and 30 inches (762 mm) in diameter at the head.

Camp Richmond, Dec. 27th

Dear Mother and Sister

I received your letter of the 21st and was very glad to hear from home and to hear that you were all well. I and all the boys are well an I hope when this reached you it will find you all the same. Mr. Bissell arrived here the evening before Christmas. I got the things you sent with him for me. We had a first rate time Christmas. The Captain furnished each mess with 6 turkeys. Then with the things the boys had gotten from home, made us quite a dinner. The fruit you sent me was very nice and I am sorry that I have nothing to send home with Mr. Bissell as a Christmas gift for any of you. I wanted the gloves for just what you thought, to wear inside my buckskins[19]. Tell Mr. Reitz that I would like to kill Jeff David but if I did I would be court marshalled by the Union officers but if I do it on the sly I will try. I would sooner have some of our Union officers strung up. We have been paid for a little over one month and I will send some home with Mr. Bissell. The weather here has been very pleasant for about three weeks. I had a letter from Frank today written on the 19th. He was well and at Nashville. The Breastworks here are completed and with out Brigade we can keep out a large force of rebels. I think we will stay here for some time, perhaps the rest of the winter. I had hoped that I would get to see Frank but we are on the wrong road. When we leave here we will be apt to go through Cumberland Gap into East Tennessee. How is our horse doing? Where is Nora Sherwood keeping house? I must bring this to a close. Give my love to all.

John Rieley

19 A form of clothing, usually consisting of a jacket and leggings, made from buckskin, a soft sueded leather from the hide of deer or elk.

Dear Mother and Sister

As we are going to move in the morning and to be on a long march, I thought I would write a few lines before we started. I don't know where we are going but I think we ill move into Tennessee. Perhaps to Nashville. We left Richmond Dec. 29th and came to this place. We came through Camp Dick Robinson[20]. It was a pretty hard looking place. I sent 15 dollars home with Mr. Bissell, did you get it? As news is very scarce here I will have to close. I am well and all the boys are the same. Direct your next to Lexington and then it will follow the Battery. Give my love to all.

John Rieley

---

[20] A Civil War encampment, recognized as the first Union base south of the Ohio River.

Dear Mother and Sister

I received yours of the 27th and was very glad to hear from home. I am well and all the boys are but Adam Glebe. He is in the hospital. He has got the typhoid fever. There is no news here of any kind. I saw a report in the paper the other day that Morgan had come into Kentucky. We were expecting to have a bush with him but he don's seem to come along. I think I won't be at the surprise party for I have not had an invitation but I would like to be there and have a set to with the floor. I think I could wear some holes in it or my boots. You can play that I am there. The time I crossed that river with my load of hay I did not wish I wasn't in Dixie[21] but I did which I was on the other side of the river. We are having some pretty cold weather here and tip-top sleighing but they don't have any cutters or sleighs of any kind. Our stable sergeant (Jim Wilson) got hurt falling from a horse. The horse was on a trot and fell throwing Wilson against a stone. He to the bridge of his nose broken. Lieutenant Smith, of our Batter, has been sick for some time with typhoid fever. He talks of retiring. I think I will retire too in a bout 30 months from now. As news is very scarce here I will bring this to a close by asking you to write soon.

Give my best wishes to all.

John Rieley

---

[21] A slang reference to the geo-political area that comprised the Confederate States of America.

Dear Mother:

You are perhaps very anxious to hear from me but not more so than I am to hear from you as the last I received was of December 18th.

You have read about the battle at this place long before this. I was in this battle and came through safe and sound. Our brigade of cavalry (the 2nd) started from Nashville with the rest of the army on the 26th of December, 1862, and went to Franklin at which place we drove them from the town, killing two, and taking twelve prisoners. From there we crossed over to a small town called Truine, where we had another fight. There were four or five of the 4th Ohio killed here. From that place, we moved on to Murfreesboro. On the 30th of December we were placed on the extreme right of the line of battle. We skirmished all day with the rebels. The next morning at two o'clock, we were ordered into our saddles and it was well that we did because we had not more than got mounted when the rebels began throwing shells into us. At daylight they advanced upon General Johnson's Division which was to the left of us who gave way and ran as fast as they could go, a great many of them throwing away their guns and leaving ten cannons to be captured by the enemy. We then had to fall back which we did in good order. We however kept the rebels in check until the infantry could get formed in our rear and then fell back. The rebel cavalry then charged our train and took possession of it, and were going to take it away with them when our regiment was ordered to charge on them and drove them off and recaptured the train. We were then ordered to guard a train through to Nashville. When we got to Laverne which is about half way, we were attacked by a brigade of rebel cavalry. We repulsed them and then went on. We stopped at Nashville one day and then returned to the battle field. We drove the rebels away and reached the battlefield that night in safety. The next day we heard that the rebels had left and our brigade was the fist troops to enter Murfreesboro after the rebels left. We have been laying in camp here since. Our regiment lost about twenty five men. Col. Milligan of the 1st Ohio was killed. Our regiment was charged seven times in one day and we were fighting for seven days and we had a hard time of it. Our company had one man wounded.

Give my regards to all.

Frank

Camp near Frankfort, Jan. 31ˢᵗ, '63

Dear Mother and Sister

I received your kind letter of the 22ⁿᵈ last night and also one from Frank of the 24ᵗʰ. He was in the fight at Murfreesboro and came out safe and sound. They charged over the rebel cavalry seven times in a day and were in the fight seven days. They had 34 killed in the Regiment. His Company had one wounded. I will not top to give you all the particulars for I suppose you will have a letter from him before this reaches you. Frank says he has not heard from home in some time. I think our Brigade will never go outside of Kentucky. We had marching twice since we have been here and the people talked to the General and got us to stay here. They are afraid of Morgan coming in and taking them. If it were not for that we would be in Murfreesboro now. Our Brigade is the only one in the State and we are bound to stay until the war is over. I am getting as fat as a hog. I weigh about a ton. I am not going to write a very long letter as I want to send it with the mail this morning. I am writing before breakfast. The boys are all well but Adam and he is not very sick. We had one many ide in the Battery this week of typhoid fever, Guy Ball, maybe you will remember him. He was in our shanty at Cleveland, a tall, slim fellow, dark complection. Write soon. Give my love to all. In much haste.

John Rieley

February 11, 1863
Murfreesboro

Dear Mother:

We are still encamped at this place.

We have to go on a scout every few days and in between we have picket duty every other day and so we are kept pretty busy and do not have much time to grumble.

We went on a scout to a small town called Liberty which is twenty nine miles east of here. Our force consisted of two brigades of infantry, two battery of artillery and one brigade of cavalry. We found that a division of infantry under Gen. Brekenridge had been camped there but had left, when he heard of our coming. We moved then to a place called Lebanon. Here the infantry camped while the cavalry went on to Rome. We came upon a small party of the Rebel cavalry. We fired a few shots and they ran. We saw some horses tied to a fence. We charged up there and who should we find but a rebel general and colonel. We took them prisoners and returned to Lebanon. The General's name was Anderson and the Colonel's was Martin. We returned to Murfreesboro.

The weather is fine and it looks like Spring was going open at once although we have had a few cold days and a little snow a week back which made me wish to be back home for a sleigh ride this Winter, but I am willing to stay in the army as long as there is a rebel with arms in his hands in the United States.

I wish for a Cleveland paper. It would be like an old friend.

Love,

Frank

Dear Mother and Sister

I received your letter of the 6th soon after date and was very glad to hear from home. I have not got much to write about buy I will let you know that I am as well as I ever was. Our Brigade is getting horses so as to have every man on a horse. We are going to be kept for the express purpose of guarding Kentucky. It will not take us long to travel all over the state. I had hoped to get into Tennessee where we would have something to do but I can't go without a pass. Guy Ball has (or at least had a father) and mother before he died. His father was sick in bed when Guy died. Guy's uncle came here and got his corpse. Things cost a big price here as well as every other place. Wood is $10 a cord[22], sugar 15 ¢ a pound, coffee 40 ¢, salt $10 a barrel, cotton cloth aint to be had at any price, milk 10 ¢ a quart, butter 45 ¢ - 50 ¢ a pound, cheese 25 ¢ a pound. A felt hat, the same as the one I brought from home costs $6 to $8 a piece. Plug tobacco[23] $1.50 a pound. I think that is pretty steep for a tobacco state. I think I could run a chance of getting a paper if you would be kind enough to send a few. We have loads of mud here. It is about four feet deep. Second Lieutenant Smith has resigned and gone home. Orderly Sargent Osterbrook has been promoted to his place. Smith has had poor health ever since we left Cleveland. There has been some resolutions passed on account of his resigning. I think you will see them in the paper. We got some new clothes the other day. We are in the 1st Brigade, 2nd Division, Army of Kentucky. They have got a new way of punishing deserters here. They brand the letter D on their left cheek. D stands for deserter. Write soon. Give my love to all.

John Rieley

19th OS[24] Army, Frankfort, Kentucky

---

[22] A measurement that corresponds to a well stacked woodpile 4 feet (122 cm) wide, 4 feet (122 cm) high, and 8 feet (244 cm) long; or any other arrangement of linear measurements that yields the same volume.

[23] A form of loose-leaf tobacco condensed with a binding sweetener that is chewed.

[24] Operational Support Army unit, frequently written as O.S. A.

Dear Mother and Sister

I received your kind letter of the 16th soon after date and was very glad to hear from home. I have not got much news to write this time. I had a letter from Frank last week. He did not write anything of importance. Things go on the same as usual in camp. Adam is no better yet. He got about over the typhoid fever when was taken down with erysipelas. His head is swelled as big as a half bushel. He is in the General Hospital in town and has first rate care. Mrs. Burrows, from the Heights, is taking care of her son. He has been sick for some time with typhoid fever. There was a battalion of the Ohio 2nd Cavalry went through here today. I think they are going to Danville. It is reported that there are 600 – 700 rebels there. The 104th and 44th Regiments went to Danville yesterday on a forced march. I thought we was going with them be we did not. I must bring my letter to a close. I will try to write a longer one next time. Write soon. Yours in much haste.

John Rieley

19th O.S.A. Frankfort, Kentucky

P.S. John Lowe sends his best respects now.

John Rieley

Dear Mother:

Was much pleased to receive a letter of February 16th.

Our regiment had a grand time over the 24th. The officers of our regiment got up a barbecue for the soldiers, celebrating Washington's Birthday. We had speechmaking by Gen. Stanley who is Chief of Cavalry in this department and Gen. Garfield of Gen. Rosecrans staff, Colonels Wagoner and Parmound and four or five captains. After the speaking was over, we went to dinner consisting of an ox roasted whole, turkey and chicken, soft bread, cheese and crackers and lastly but not least six barrels of beer and plenty of cigars. The 4th regiment band played for us all day and most of the night. The turkey and chicken, we confiscated out in the country and the ox we captured and roasted ourselves. The soft bread as we call it was quite a treat to us after living on hard crackers so long.

There have been some changes among our officers. Col. Zahn has resigned and Major Paramound has been promoted to Colonel and 1st Lieutenant of our Company Clark Center has been discharged, Lieutenant Col. D.A. Murray, Majors Foster, Sidell and Howland, Capt. Of our Company, H.B. Gaylord, 1st Lieut. Fred Breman and 2nd Lieut. G. B. Watson.

I expect to be paid today and will send it as before.

My brother John wrote that he could beat me in weight but he will have to eat more hard crackers as he weighs 185 lbs. and I weigh 195 lbs.

Send some more postage stamps, etc.

Love,

Frank

Dear Mother and Sister

I now take my pen in hand to write you a few lines to let you know that I am alive and kicking. I have not had a letter from home in some time. I got one paper last week and I think you sent a letter to me with it. If you did, I have not got it. Since I last wrote home we have had a great deal of excitement here. On the 23rd of February a report came into Frankfort that there was a large force of rebels marching on the town. Our Section of the Battery was ordered out to guard the turnpike coming into town. We stayed there all night waiting patiently for Johnny Rebel to arrive but he didn't come. On the 26th we left Frankfort in the evening about dark and came through to Lexington on a forced march. We were looking for a brush with the rebels when we got here. I suppose they heard of the 19th Ohio Battery coming in and they lit out. Captain Shield has been home on a furlough. He got back this morning and I never saw a better pleased lot of boys than the boys of the Battery. They gave him three rousing cheers that made the country ring for miles around. If there were any rebels near it would have scared them out of the State. Adam was left in Frankfort. There was a man came from there yesterday and he said that Adam was getting better. He is able to e out of bed and walk around. The rest of the boys are all well and I never felt better. You must write soon. No more for now. Give my love to all.

John Rieley

P.S. Here is a letter Albert Bishop is sending to James Skinner.

March 23, 1863
Camp near Murfreesboro

Dear Mother:

A long time since I heard from home – last was of February 16th. However I have received two papers which were welcome.

We have a brush with the rebels every few days now. About the 1st of the month, our brigade went to a small town called Bradyville which is eighteen miles south of here where there was a brigade of cavalry. When we were three miles from the town, we were met by their pickets which we drove in and then formed in line of battle and charged on them. The rebels were on top of a hill which was very rocky and covered with trees and as we came up the side of the hill, they gave us a volley which made us go back but soon rallied and drove them from the hill. We took about one hundred and fifty prisoners and thirty killed and wounded. Our brigade lost four men killed and ten wounded. Our Company had one man wounded. We then returned to Murfreesboro.

The next day we went on another scout westward about twenty miles. The first brigade which was in advance came upon a lot of rebel cavalry. Our boys charged the rebels and drove them like sheep, capturing sixty prisoners and the camp equipment of the regiment. We scouted around that country for a few days and then went to Franklin and then south to the place where Col. Couburne and his brigade was captured. Here we had a skirmish with Van Dorn cavalry. We took about twenty prisoners. After that we went on to Duck river having two or three skirmishes with the rebels and then returned to Franklin and then to Murfreesboro having been gone twelve days.

Love

Frank

Dear Mother and Sister

I once more take my pen in hand to write you a few lines. I received your letter of Mar. 6th and also one of the 20th, that can of horse radish and a paper. The horse radish was the best treat I have had in some time. I expect that you will begin to think I have quit writing all together. Well I had a great notion to quite but I thought it would be most too hard on you. We have been working on our fortification here for the last few days. It was the hardest work I have done since I left home and then it was not very hard for we only worked 5 or 6 hours a day. Our forces have been skirmishing with the rebels for the last 8 to 10 days but I haven't seen a rebel since I left home. I think I will run a chance of seeing some this summer for they are making great preparations to give us a visit. We will try to give them a warm reception. The troops are just rushing in here from the northern states. They come in here at a rate of 4 or 5 thousand a day. I suppose we are going to have a large Army in this state. Al Bishop had a letter from Andy last week. He said they had orders to march for this place. We are looking every day to see him. The 6th New York Regiment came in here the other day. It is the Regiment that did the big fighting at Bull Run. The 4th Ohio Battery is here. This is the Battery that Edward Pritchard is in. I saw him the other day but did not speak to him. I suppose he would feel too big to speak to me if he knew me. Adam is in the hospital at Frankfort yet. He is not getting much better. John Bissell said that unexpected letter was a very interesting one. I think so myself. Well I must bring my letter to a close. The boys are all well and I never felt better. Tell Mr. Reitz that I would like to go over to Peats with him and take a glass of lager. Give my best regards to anyone that may enquire about me.

John Rieley

Camp near Nashville
April 4, 1863

Dear Mother and Friends:

I have at last reached the regiment I went from Cleveland to Shelby with and then learned that the regiment had started for Nashville Tuesday morning. I got on the cars again and went to Columbus. There I found a lot of new recruits who were going to start for the regiment that same night and I went with them. We reached Cincinnati the next morning at 3:00 A.M. and at 12:00 o'clock left for Louisville on steamboat "Prima Donna," reaching Louisville at 9:00 o'clock A.M. We laid in Louisville until 4:00 P.M. when we started for Nashville on the cars and reached there at daylight the next morning, the 3rd. Joined the regiment which is a mile and a half west of Nashville. Nothing was said because I stayed long than I ought to have stayed.

All the boys are back except two sick with smallpox and one who died. Nearly all had a spell of sickness while on furlough. I felt like sleeping last night for the first time since I left home. It is a very disagreeable day and one not calculated to give a fellow a high opinion of the beauties of camp life. It has rained all night and is still drizzling, but all we can do is to sit in the "dog tents" and "let it rain."

Our regiment got a great many recruits while at home and now has eleven hundred men. Our Company has one hundred twenty five men. The 1st Ohio and the 4th Ohio are camped here with us having just returned from home. I am well and feel first rate.

As I have nothing more to write I will close, but hold on I had forgot one thing. That fellow that had my overcoat took it to Shelby, Ohio and not finding me took it to Columbus, from there sent it to Cleveland by expressed, addressed Frank Rieley. You will find the ticket enclosed. Please go to the Express Office and get it at American Express on Bank St. Write soon addressing me Co. I 3rd O 2C Nashville, Tenn.

Give my best respects to all.

Frank Rieley

Camp near Lexington Apr. 7

Dear Mother and Sister

I received your letter of the 6th yesterday and was glad to hear from home. I have not got much news to write this time. There is some talk of us leaving here to go to Nashville but I guess it is nothing but a camp rumor. If it will help to wind this war up and sooner I would like to go down there any how. Well, Mary, you spoke of coming down here to give me a visit this summer. I would like first rate to see you but I think it would be a great deal better for you to stay home. If you came down here you would have to stop in town at some boarding house and I could not leave camp to hunt one up for you. I cannot leave camp for ten minutes at a time. If you wore breeches you might come right into camp and stay here until you got ready to go home again. I don't think you would like to go to all that trouble. You asked me how I liked Captain Wilson – well Wilson has not got to be Captain yet and there is no prospect of him getting to be either. He is just Commander of the Battery in Captain Shield's absence. Shields is around here every day and sees that everything is kept straight and when we leave here (if we ever do) Captain Shields is going with us. We had a man desert a few days ago, his name is Reed, he was gone five days and then came back on his own hook. We have a Battery drill every day. We drill about three hours a day. The other day when we was out drilling there was a New York editor looking at and he said that he never saw a better looking lot of men in one Battery since the war first broke out. The Burg Boys are all well and I never felt better. Give my best respects to anyone that things enough of me to inquire how I am. Yours in much haste.

John Rieley

P.S. John Bissell has just got a letter from home. He said his father got that money. Did you get that record I sent home? That box has not get here yet. I expect it will be here today.

John Rieley

71

Murfreesboro, Tenn.
April 13, 1863

Dear Mother and friends:

I received your letter of March 23ᵈ a few days ago and was much pleased to hear from home, and to hear that you were all well. It is some time since I heard from brother John. The postage stamps were very acceptable and also the papers. I received three of them and they looked like old friends. I wrote you a letter about the 26ᵗʰ. Did you receive it?

A few days after that we went on a scout to Liberty, a small town twenty nine miles east of here. When we go within nine miles of the town, we came onto a small force of rebels. We drove them two or three miles and it being dark we camped for the night. The next morning, we again started on, when about two miles from town, we came across another small body of rebels. We gave them a few shots and they then fell back. We then advanced and got two miles beyond the town when the rebels appeared upon us with six pieces of artillery. Our forces consisted of about two thousand cavalry, a brigade of infantry and six pieces of artillery, the whole commanded by General Stanley. Our artillery soon opened on the rebels in front. The 3ᵈ and 4ᵗʰ OC were sent around to the rear of the rebels. The country was very hilly. We had to climb on three hills leading our horses. The 4ᵗʰ Ohio Cavalry was in advance and soon came upon the rebels in thick woods. The 4ᵗʰ Ohio dismounted and fought the rebels for about a half hour, driving them from the woods. Our regiment was ordered to charge which we did, driving the rebels like sheep before us for a couple of miles. Seeing that we were outnumbered about five to one, we thought best to stop, and wait for the rest of our force to come up. We waited for a while, when we were ordered back. We took thirty or forty prisoners, a lot of mules and horses and eight or ten wagons. We went back about ten miles and camped for the night. The next day we went to Lebanon and then returned to Murfreesboro.

Our regiment is now on a scout, but our Company was on picket duty and not taken. The 2ᵈ battalion of our regiment is out at Readyville, twelve miles southeast of here with General Hagen's brigade. They had a fight there not long ago. I suppose you saw an account of it in the papers. I do not know how long it will be before we move from this place, but I guess not long and when we do, we will march on to another victory. I have strong hopes of getting home by next Fall if the "butternuts" in the north will only keep still and stop their everlasting cry of "This is a nigger war" and "Peace at any price." I think the easiest way to settle this is to whip the rebels and then and not till then will there be peace. But enough of this.

I will send with this letter a piece cut from the Ohio State Journal²⁵ printed at Columbus, Ohio, in which is an account of the proceedings in our regiment at

---

25 The *Ohio State Journal* was the Republican Party's (the party of President Abraham Lincoln) main voice in central Ohio during the Civil War years.

the funeral of one of our Company who died of wounds received at Bradyville in a skirmish and account of which I wrote in my last letter. I will also send you by mail a copy of the Nashville Union, which may be interesting to you.

The weather is warm at present, but we have had some cold spells which felt very much like the weather at home. The peach trees were in blossom some time ago and now all the trees are budding out and looks very much like Spring.

I am fat and hearty as usual owing I suppose to the plenty full way Uncle Sam supplies us with hard tack and sow belly as we call hard bread and bacon.

If you find any fault with this letter, you can't grumble because it is not long enough.

I want you to write a long letter even if you have no news to write.

Love to all the family.

Yours truly,

Frank Rieley

Camp Clay, April 23rd

Dear Mother and Sister

I thought I would write you a few lines to keep you from forgetting that I am away from home and down here in Kentucky. As it is long since I heard from home I though you had forgotten already. Yours of the 6th is the last letter I received. I answered that as soon as I received it. In your last letter you spoke of having to go to the Post Office every day or two and back without a letter, well I don't that is my fault so much as your own. Last month there was a time when I did not get a letter for two weeks and I said I would not write for a month if I did not get one the next week. Well I did not get one the next week or for some time after that but I wrote before my month was out. That was the only time I recollect of not writing regular or as soon as I had time. We moved our camp yesterday. We are in Clay's farm near our old camp. We have been assigned to the Army of Central Kentucky. I suppose we will stay here all summer. Some of our men was opening a shell the other day and the powder took fire and burned and wounded three of our men.   H.W. Redhead, our blacksmith, Mr. V. Leeper and George Patterson. They are all doing well. I suppose you will know Leeper. If you don't just ask Lib Bishop. We had a heavy rain last night and were all like to get drowned. Did you get that money I sent home and that record. I got them things you sent me. The paper and envelopes got a little wet from the horse radish bursting in the box but they are not spoiled. That tobacco Mr. Reitz sent me was just the thing I wanted. The Burgh boys are all well and so am I. Give my best respects to Mr. Reitz. I will close by asking you to write soon.

John Rieley

Camp Stanley
Murfreesboro, Tenn.
April 29, 1863

Dear Mother and friends:

I received your letter of April 24th a day or so ago and was much pleased to hear from home. I have not had any letters from Brother John for some time. Since my last letter, we have been on another scout down to Dixie. On the 20th we started from Murfreesboro. Our force consisted of about fifteen hundred cavalry, one thousand mounted infantry and a brigade of infantry and ten pieces of artillery. The cavalry was under command of Col. Minty and the whole under command of Gen. Reynolds. The first day we went to Readyville, twelve miles southeast. We camped there for the night. The next morning at 1:00 o'clock we advanced toward McMinnville. When we had advanced twelve miles, the 3rd and 4th O.C. and part of a Tennessee regiment left the pike and went to the right in the direction of the railroad which runs from Tullahoma to McMinnville. After a long ride of twenty or thirty miles, we at last reached the railroad. We formed in line and waited for a train. After a wait of fifteen minutes, we heard a train whistle a couple of miles from us in the direction of Tullahoma[26]. This made our eyes glisten and our hearts beat faster, as we waited for it to come within reach of us. After waiting an hour or more, we came to the conclusion that someone must have stopped it and told them that the "Yankees" were in that vicinity. When we found that the train would not come, we burned a bridge and then went along the track toward McMinnville. After going a couple of miles, we came onto another train which was standing at the station called Moristown. We saw five or six men running away but we soon made them prisoners. From them we learned that the "Yankees" were in McMinnville also and that the rebels had run the train out for safety thinking that they could get to Tullahoma but had run into another lot of Yankees. We burned the train and again started for McMinnville. When we got within four or five miles of the town, we camped for the night. The next day, we went to McMinnville. When our forces went into the town, the day before they took about one hundred fifty prisoners destroyed commissary stores, a large cotton factory, cotton, etc. An account of which you have seen in the papers probably. From McMinnville, we went to Liberty and then west to Alexandria where we burnt a flour mill. We then returned to McMinnville having been away seven days.

You asked if that man who was buried was an officer – No he was a private, and we think as much of every man and a great deal more of some men in our regiment. We have been paid since I wrote that we were going to be paid, but I could get no way to send money home that I thought would be safe, so I

---

[26] Tullahoma, located in south-central Tennessee, was then little more than a rough outpost, with no paved streets. 1863 was a wet year, and the place became known to the bedraggled troops of both sides as a place of endless mud. One witty officer on Confederate General William Hardee's staff is said to have written his own account of the origin of the name: "It is from two Greek words - 'Tulla' meaning mud, and 'Homa,' meaning more mud."

kept it. I think I can get a furlough sometime this Summer and tell Tommy and Sylvester that I will bring them some "hard tack" and "sow belly" then.

You ask did I ever see this fellow. Well after standing for three or four hours, I came to the conclusion that I had and that it was my big brother. Has Willie got well of that bruise yet and is he able to work?

The weather is very warm here in the daytime, but cold at night and when we are out of camp and no tents, our overcoats are very comfortable yet. I must close as I have written too much already.

Give my love to all the family.

Very truly yours,

Frank Rieley

Camp near Murfreesboro,
May 7, 1863

Dear Mother:

I sent home with this letter ten dollars by express, you will have to pay the express charges on it.

Some of our regiment are going to Louisville after horses and I will send it with them and have them send it from there.

Am in good health. I hear the 2ᵈ OVC will come here in a few days.

I had a letter from brother John a few days ago. He is well.

Write soon and oblige,

Frank Rieley

Camp near Murfreesboro, Tenn.
May 16, 1863

Dear Mother:

I received your letter of the 12th today and was very glad to hear from home and also that you were all well. I received a letter from brother John a few days ago. There has nothing of interest happened in this regiment lately.

We went to Levergne and staid there three days. Levergne was once a town between Nashville and Murfreesboro, but it is now burned to the ground. The reason we went there was that we expect the rebel General Wheeler with his cavalry was going to attack the railroad at that place. He did not come and we returned to Murfreesboro.

The weather is very fine there, but almost too warm in the day time, and too cold at night. It seems strange to me that we do not move forward from this place but I suppose "Old Rosey" (Rosencrans) knows his business. I think when we do move, we will give a better account of ourselves than the Potomac army does.

I am sorry to hear that you have so much trouble at home. I think I can get a furlough this Summer and then I can straighten things out. In the meantime, do the best you can. A week ago, I sent home thirty dollars by express as some of our Company were going to Louisville and instructed them to express to Hugh Rieley, care J.B. Smith, Cleveland. And if you have not gotten it, go there and get it and pay charges.

Write soon and give my love to all the family.

Frank Rieley

Dear Mother and Sister

I received your kind letter of the 22nd today and was much pleased to hear from home again and to hear that the folks were all well. We have moved our camp since I last wrote home. We are in our old camp again where we were last fall. How does Willie like to work at his trade? What men does Mr. Reitz get to work for him and what does he pay his best man? Who was that best man who left Mr. Reitz? I think we will leave here soon and I will get a chance to kill Jeff and I think that when is out of the way we will get home soon so I may help Reitz to get some of that work out of the way. You spoke of meeting a furlough, well, there has been 5 or 6 men trying to get one for some time but it was no go. Adam has not got his discharge and I don't think he will get one either. He is in the hospital in Cincinnati. One of the boys had a letter from him. He said he would be with us again soon. I think Frank Stockle has done first rate. John Bissell fell from a horse wagon today and hurt himself. He Is not very bad though for he is walking around the camp. There is great excitement in camp over the news from Vicksburg and one many has two months pay bet that it is in our possession. I think if it aint now it will be and when it is taken I think I can see and end of this war but I may have to look five or six months ahead. I want you to have a good Christmas dinner ready next Christmas for I think that us soldier boys will be home at that time. The weather here is very warm and dry. There is no lake breeze here. I must bring my letter to a close by asking you to write soon. Be sure to write soon.

John Rieley

Camp Turchin,
Murfreesboro,
June 8, 1863

Dear Mother and Friends"

I received your letter of May 30ᵗʰ a few days ago and was much pleased to hear from home. I have not had a letter from John in some time. Everything goes on as usual at this place.

Our brigade was on another scout and we have just got back. We were out to Liberty again. Our Brigade of Cavalry and a brigade of mounted infantry started from here on the 4ᵗʰ and wen tot Liberty without meeting the enemy. We camped for the night and the next morning went to Smithville. When near that place, we ran into pickets. We drove them in, but they would not fight and ran from town into the woods and commenced bush whacking us as we advanced, but the infantry came up and soon drove the bush whackers out of the woods. We had two pieces of artillery along and got into position and gave the rebels some shells one of which we after learned killed on many and five horses. The rebels did not trouble us after that. We then went back to Liberty and staid two days and then returned to Murfreesboro.

The boys here are all in good spirits and eager for a fight and I guess we will soon have a chance to fight for I think "Old Rosey" will not lay still much longer.

The weather is getting pretty warm at this place. It is as warm here now as at home in July and August.

I saw my friend, John Holler, the other day in the 10ᵗʰ OVC. He looks well. The 10ᵗʰ OVC is in our brigade. But I must bring this letter to a close.

Give my love to all the family and write soon,

Yours truly,

Frank Rieley

I wish that you would send some envelopes. Do them up like a newspaper and they will come through.

Frank

Dear Mother and Sister

I received your kind letter of the 3rd a day or two since and was much pleased to hear from home. I wrote a letter home a week ago. Did you get it with $15 dollars in it? Adam is with us again and he looks first rate and all the boys that you know in the Battery (myself with them) are in as good health as ever we was and I hope when this reaches home it will find you all the same. Since I last wrote home we have been on the move near all the time. We got here to Somerset, part of the 2nd Ohio Cavalry and parts of two or three other Regiments was across the Cumberland River fighting the rebels. There was quite a number killed and wounded on both sides. Andrew Bishop was among the latter. We was only wounded slightly. He got a buckshot[27] just below his elbow. The ball is in the arm yet and he is doing first rate. The 2nd is in camp next to us. We have a first rate camp here in the woods with the best spring of water that you ever saw only 500 yards from camp. Out tents were turned over to the Quarter Master the other day and he gave us some dog tents in place of them. I will give you a description of them for I suppose you have never saw any of them. Well they are made of cotton cloth and when it rains the water comes through them like it would through a sieve. They are made for two to sleep in (Albert Bishop and I sleep together). Well if you take a sheet off the bed there at home and take it out in the garden and get two sticks about three feet long and drive them into the ground about six feet apart, then put another stick six feet long on the top of the ones driven into the ground. Spread the sheet onto it and put a small stake at each corner so as to keep it spread out with each end open and you will have a god tent like the one I am laying in trying to write this letter. I will close by asking you to write soon. Be sure to write soon.

John Rieley

John Rieley
19th Battery O.L.A.
Somerset, Ky.
Care of Captain J.C. Shields

---

[27] Buckshot is large shotgun pellet that must be carefully packed into a shell rather than simply being poured in, and it typically used for hunting large game, such as deer.

Camp Carter, June 18, 1863

Dear Mother and Sister

I received your kind letter of the 14th yesterday and was pleased to hear from home again. We are going on a march in the morning and I think it will be a long one for we have around ten days rations to start with. I think we will go east into Tennessee but that is only a thought. They don't let such as me know anything about such orders. All the troops in this place are on the march in the morning. We were called out this morning at 3 o'clock and was going to leave at daybreak but we did not get away but are sure to go in the morning. Andrew Bishop is getting along first rate. He was here this afternoon and said he was going to Hickmans Bridge. He was going to start at 4 P.M. Hickmans Bridge is 20 miles this side of Lexington. All the sick and wounded in this place are going to the same place. Andrew thinks they will go through to Camp Dennison. We have been tieing up our extra clothing such as overcoats, blankets, etc. that we don't want only this winter and are going to send them back to Lexington until next fall. I sent that big quilt (the one I took when I left home) back. I received them stamps you sent me. I now have a lot on hand. If I happen to want any I won't be anyways backward to send for some. That mess we had with our Lieutenant has all quieted down and he gets along first rate now. You wanted to know if us boys would like to be home to spend the 4th well I would like to be there first rate if this was over but I don't want to go home as long as there is a rebel in arms in the United States which I think won't be long. I think they are making their last desperate struggle. You can direct your letters the same as you have been doing. I think it will be some time until you hear from me again but I will write at the first opportunity. You must write soon. Give my love to all the family.

John Rieley

Dear Mother and Sister

I received yours of the 27ᵗʰ a few days ago and was very much pleased to hear from home again. It may be some time before you get letters from me for the rebels are between here and Lexington. Our Battery is in the Army of Central Kentucky commanded by General Burnside. We are not attached to any Brigade or Division that I know of. There was some talk of being attached to General Mott's Brigade but I think this is just a camp rumor. We did not go on that march that I spoke of when I last wrote home. We spend the 4ᵗʰ at Somerset and it was pretty dull. We fired a salute of 21 guns in the morning at sunrise, 35 at noon and 21 at sunset. We fired 35 at noon for the 35 states. It rained the entire week we were in Somerset so we were pretty well soaked when we left there on the 5ᵗʰ. It is 35 miles from Somerset to this place but the way the road was when we came through it must have been 60 miles. The mud was up to the hubs of our gun wheels nearly all the way. It was the roughest road I ever saw. We had to run over rocks sometimes and then over logs and then in the mud again up to our necks. First one capsized then another and a mule wagon tipped over and so on all the way. We lived old high all the time we were in Somerset. We used to go nearly every night and get a hog or a sheep. In the daytime we picked black berries and milked the father's cows. Then they said we were not half as bad as the rebs for they said they would milk the cows and then take all the cows, horses, and hogs the people had and burn them out because they had no more. I think Stanford is the prettiest little place I was ever in. The crops look first rate here, the wheat is nearly all cut. Andrew Bishop is at Camp Dennison and doing first rate. Albert had a letter from him the other day. I must bring this to a close and brush some of the mud off my clothes for it is just getting dry after our march. Give my best respects to Mr. and Mrs. Reitz. Write soon.

John Rieley

Camp near Winchester[28]
July 9th, 1863

Dear Mother:

I received your kind letter of the 20th, a few days ago.

You have probably heard of the movement in this Department long before this. Well we have had considerable skirmishing with the rebels since we left Murfreesboro. Our regiment had one man killed and eight men wounded. We are now stuck in the mud. It having rained every day since we started but one. We are camped about five miles from Winchester and forty miles from Huntsville, Ala., waiting for rations. We have had pretty hard times lately, having been seven days without rations. What little we had to eat we got from Secesh farmers. I expect that you can get much better accounts of the movements from papers than I can give you. I will write again as soon as the mail route is open.

Our Colonel Paramore has been dismissed from the service by General Rosecrans for disobedience of orders, and he is going home and I will send this letter with him; as it the only chance we will have to send mail for some time.

We hear that Vicksburg has been taken and that the rebel army in Penn. has been cut to pieces by Hooker, but we do not know whether to believe it or not. If it is so, it is good news.

But I must close this hastily written letter and ask that your write soon.

I am in the 2nd Brigade, 2nd Division Cavalry Command. Direct letters to Tullahoma, Tenn.

Yours in haste,

Frank

---

28 A town located in southern Tennessee, near the border with Alabama.

McConnellsville[29], July 27, '63

Dear Mother and Sister

I one more seat myself to write you a few lines. We left Hamilton the 17th for Cincinnati and arrived the same day. We went into camp the next morning. We started to Marrietta by rail road 200 miles. We came through Chillicothe and the people of that town got us a first rate dinner and gave us about a wagon load of bread and cheese to take with us. We only stopped there 20 minutes then went on to Marietta where we arrived on the 20th. If we stopped five minutes on the road the people would be seen running from all directions to us with grub for us. We stayed in Marrietta a few days and then our section of the Battery was ordered up the Musgingum River on a steam boat in search of Morgan. We arrived at this place yesterday morning which is 56miles from Marrietta. Morgan was up the river 8 miles crossing when we arrived here. We got our guns off the boat and took after him as fast as our horses could go. When we got there he had got across the river with his whole force. We went about two miles up the hills and found him in a hollow in the woods. We gave him a few shots and he stared on a keen jump. We followed him about two miles and got a few more shots off at him but our horses were so tired out that they could not overtake him. There were 21 rebels dead found in the fields, one man killed and one wounded on our side before we came up. The rebels did not stop to fire a single shot after they heard the road of our artillery. We are encamped in the center of town and the ladies are feeding us like fighting cocks. I think they are just trying to see which of them can get up the best meals and the most soldiers to eat them. For every meal there are six or seven invitation for each one of us to go and eat. I think it will be near as hard for me to leave here as it would be for me to leave home. We leave this evening for Marietta. This is the third letter I have written home and have not got an answer to any of them yet and think you had better not write until we get settled down someplace. Don't write until you hear from me again for I won't get it if you do. I must close for I must pack up my dry goods and get ready to leave. You must excuse this for my pencil is not very good. Give my love to all the family.

John Rieley

[29] The town in Ohio that was the northernmost point penetrated by the Confederate Army during Morgan's Civil War Raid June 11 – July 26, 1863

Camp Winchester, Tenn.
August 4, 1863

Dear Mother and friends:

I received your kind letter of July 22nd a few days ago, and was much pleased to hear from you, once more.

We were paid about a week ago and I will send this with $60.00 by express to J.B. Smith. We were paid for four months up to June 30th. Rosecran's army is still in the same position it was when I wrote you last. The army laying at Winchester, Dechard and Cowan's Station. The cavalry is kept busy however skirmishing and scouting through the country. Since I last wrote, we have been to New Market and Huntsville, Ala. Elkton and Pulaski and Fayetteville, Tenn. At the latter place, we staid about a week and did a big business gathering in "Niggers" and mules. The Niggers I hear are to be organized into regiments and armed. We returned to this place yesterday. Gen. Tuchin has been relieved of the command of this division the 2nd, and the command given to Gen. Crook. I think we will soon move on to Chattanooga, but I don't think they will fight there as they have a habit of running lately.

I see by the papers that the Ohio people have had lively times with Morgan lately and have to him caged at last. You may be sure that we felt a little thankful when we got the news and we would like to have been there to settle old scores. I wonder how he likes his room in the Penitentiary.

We are all in good spirits and anxious to be moving, and finish up the war and get home. Everything looks bright and I think a few more victories for us will wind the war up. If all our generals were like Grant, it would be ended before this time. The weather is very warm here and not very comfortable marching in the hot sun.

When you get this letter, let me know if the money got home safe. I received the envelopes. Excuse this hastily written letter and give my love to all the family..

Frank Rieley

Camp near Bridgeport
August 27th, 1863

Dear Mother and Friends:

I received your welcome letter of the 13th about a week ago. I should have answered it sooner but we have been on the march from Winchester to this place. We left Winchester on the 19th. We being the last of Rosecran's army that left that place. All the Infantry and Artillery went ahead of us. We had to cross a mountain which was very steep and rocky but we got over safe and sound. We are about a mile from the Tennessee River. Our picket being on the bank of the north side and the rebel picket on the other side.

I expect we will have pretty hard times when we attempt to cross the river, but I guess they will skedaddle when we cone get on the other side. I think the army will move in about a week.

I see by the papers that Burnside's army is moving south and as brother John is in his army, I may have a chance to see him, as I think Burnside will join Rosecrans. The soldiers here are in fine spirits at the prospects of a fight.

I have nothing worth writing at present but I expect times will change before long in this department.

You ask what I think of the Niggers. Well I think they make firstrate soldiers although not as good as white men yet.

There is a rumour that fort Sumter has fallen. Glorious news if true. I must close. Direct your letters to Stevenson, Ala. Please send a few postage stamps if you can.

Yours truly,

Frank Rieley

Knoxville, Sept. 8th, 1863

Dear Mother and Sister

I suppose that you think I am not going to write home at all for I have not wrote home in over two weeks. I have been waiting to see if I would not get a letter from home before writing and I have expecting one every day for over a month. The last one I received was written on the 13th of August. This is the 4th one I have written since I received that one. I also sent home some papers. I wish you would write and let me know if you got them. There is no news here of any kind to write therefore I will not write you a very long letter this time. We are still on half rations and the prospects are good for remaining so but you must not think that we are starving for the half rations is more than I ever ate at home and then I thought I was a big eater and I guess you did too. The last letter I wrote home I told you that were going to move the next morning but we did not go. When did you hear from Frank? I have not heard from him in two months and I would like to hear how he came out in the last big fight they had. We don't get any papers here so we don't know what is going on in the rest of the world. The weather here has been very cold for the last few days, so cold that they boys would crowd around the camp fires to keep warm. It has been colder than it was a year ago when we were in Cleveland. We are going to have a chance to vote next Tuesday. I have seen any of the tickets yet but the Captain has got some here. I don't care about voting only against "traitor" Valandigham[30]. I must bring this letter to a close. I wish you would send me a few postage stamps. You must write soon. Give my best respects to all the family. The Burgh boys are all well.

John Rieley

---

[30] Clement Laird Vallandigham (July 29, 1820 – June 17, 1871) was an Ohio politician, and leader of the Copperhead faction of anti-war Democrats during the American Civil War. Vallandigham openly criticized Lincoln's preliminary Emancipation Proclamation.

Tennessee

Camp near Knoxville,

Sept. 15, 1863

Dear Mother and Sister

As I have a few spare moments I thought I would improve them by writing a few lines home to let you know that I in the land of the living. I had to write the last letter I wrote home in such a hurry that I not have time to tell you what kind of place Knoxville was when our troops first came here. The people here are better Union people than I ever saw in Ohio but when we came in here the most of the men sere out among the mountains and caves and in one place or another where ever they could best hide to keep out of the rebel conscription. I was talking to one young man here the other day I asked him how he kept out of the rebel conscription and he told me he had been hid in the mountains for the last eleven months. He never was more than a half a mile from home and had not been home but one or two times and he did not stay more than 5 minutes each time. Knoxville is a quite a fine town. There is a railroad runs through here from Nashville to Richmond and steam boats run up here in the Tennessee River. I suppose we will take the bridge on the railroad 20 miles from here 1-1/4 miles long that the rebels burned before they left. Our men have been to work building it up ever since we came here. It will be done in a few days when trains will run from Nashville to here. I suppose you heard of the surrender of Cumberland Gap before this one section of our Battery was up there and the boys say it would have been a pretty hard place to take if the rebs had took a notion to fight but our boys say they were most all conscripts and would not fight. Captain Shields has been under arrest for a few days. The boys say it was for refusing to obey one of General Hartsiffs orders but I suppose he will come out allright yet. Well I must bring this letter to a close. Did you get that letter and them papers that I sent home from here? I forgot to tell you in my last letter where to direct your next to but I hope you have not delayed in writing or they would come to me here if they was directed most anyplace in Kentucky. Direct your next to 19th Battery O.L.A. Army Corps, East Tennessee. I expect we will leave here in a few days. Write soon.

John Rieley

P.S. We leave in the morning for a big salt works 140 miles from here in Virginia. When we take it the rebels can't get any.

The boys are all well and so am I.

John

Dear Mother and friends:

I received your letter of the 10th a few days ago. I am very glad to hear from home.

A hard battle has just been fought ten miles south of Chattanooga and we have been compelled by over three times our number of rebels to fall back to this place. I think however that the rebels have got the worst of the fight. At least two corps of Lee's army were in the Battle of Chicamauga[31]. Rosecran's army fought them bravely for three days but found it impossible to whip the whole southern confederacy. Our army is in a strong position around Chattanooga. The cavalry are all on this side guarding the fords along the river. Our brigade had a hard fight on Sunday last and lost about one hundred fifty men killed and wounded. The brigade charged on a body of rebel cavalry, when they broke to the left and right they uncovered a long line of rebel infantry eight deep who let a volley into them which told with deadly effect on our boys. My horse had given out the day before and I was not in the fight. I have since gotten another horse and am again ready to fight the rebel crew. The rebels have invested Chattanooga and skirmishing is going on all the time night and day. Last night at 11 o'clock Longstreet's Corps made a charge on Renhold's Division but was repulsed with heavy loss. We expect to have reinforcements from Burnside and Grant. Some reinforcements have already come in one brigade of Burnside's Army.

Can you tell me what Division Brother John is in. It is almost impossible to find anybody here unless you know what Division he is in.

I have had not chance to see the 41st yet, but I am anxious to see the Bang Boys in that regiment.

Most of the infantry regiments were cut up awfully.

I think we will soon have another battle at this place. It may take place any day.

I must close. Give my love to all the family and write soon.

Frank Rieley

---

[31] The Battle of Chickamauga, fought September 19–20, 1863,[1] marked the end of a Union offensive in southeastern Tennessee and northwestern Georgia called the Chickamauga Campaign. The battle was the most significant Union defeat in the Western Theater of the American Civil War.

Dear Mother and friends:

I received your letter of October 12ᵗʰ about a week ago but have not had an opportunity until now of writing. We have had busy times since I wrote last, having been after Wheeler's Cavalry.

We left Chatanooga and went up the river[32] about thirty miles when our Company and Company C was left at a place called PennysFord to guard the fort. We had been there a day or so when we got word that the rebel cavalry had crossed the river up about thirty miles from where we were. We then joined the regiment and the regiment started on to join the brigade which was in pursuit of the rebels. We traveled forty six miles the first day but the rebel brigade was still twenty miles ahead. We started on the morning and came up with them about noon. We were then six miles from McMinnville and we had good reason to believe the rebels were in that place. We advanced and got into that place just as the rear guard of the rebels were leaving. The rebels had captured four hundred men and a lot of commissary stores at this place. The rebels had gone toward Murfreesboro and we followed, overtaking their rear guard about six miles from town. We had a brisk fight until dark. We went into camp for the night. We started in the morning, but the rebels had marched all night and got out of the way. We got to Murfreesboro but the rebels marched around it fearing the big guns at the fort.

We drew three days rations at Murfreesboro on October 6ᵗʰ which was the first rations we had received since the 19ᵗʰ when we got three days from Murfreesboro. We went to Shelbyville and then our division went towards Farmington which is a small town twenty miles west of Shelbyville. When we got about eight miles from Shelbyville, Wilder's Brigade of the mounted infantry came up with the rebel rear guard, Wilder's men dismounted and advanced on the rebels when they found a whole brigade drawn up, our boys gave the rebels a couple of volleys from their seven shooters, when the rebels commenced falling back. The 3ʳᵈ O was ordered to charge which we did driving them five miles and taking three hundred prisoners. They then opened six pieces of artillery on us and we were obliged to face back out of range and wait for the infantry. They soon came up and our artillery opened up on them and Wilder's men charged on them and after a short fight captured four pieces of artillery. This ended the fight as it was almost night. The fight lasted four hours. Our loss was sixty killed and wounded. Our Company had one man and one 2ⁿᵈ Lieu wounded. My horse was shot but I soon captured another. We captured four hundred prisoners, four pieces of cannon and ten wagons. After that we pursued them to the Tennessee River but they marched all night and got out of the way. We however captured one hundred more at the river. We started back through Pulaske, Fayetteville, Salem, New Market and Mysville, Ala. We are now in our old camp where

---

[32] The Tennessee River.

we camped fourteen months ago but I must close. I received those stamps which I asked you for. Love to all the family and write soon.

Frank Rieley

Knoxville, Nov. 1, 1863

Dear Mother and Sister

I received your most welcome letter of (the one Ma wrote on August 25th) and yours of Sept. 26th. I received them about a week since and you had better believe I was glad to hear from home again for I had not heard from home in two months. I suppose you will think I had ought to have wrote home sooner but I have been at work every day for about three weeks building a stable for our horses and log huts for us to winter in. John Bissell, Bishop, John Pease, Adam Glebe and myself are in a hut by ourselves. Our hut is 12 feet long, 8 feet wide and 6 feet high. We have a good fireplace to build a fire in so if they let us remain here over winter and give us plenty to eat we will be just as comfortable as if we were at home. We have been on half rations ever since we came into this state. I did not know what is was to soldier before we came into this state and then we don't have it near so bad as most of the soldiers for we have been laying here in camp ever since we came to Knoxville. Most all the rest of the soldiers have been running around. Our Battery is so heavy that we cannot run around much. I am sorry to hear of Willie and Reitz having any trouble. I know he always used me first rate and I never want a better man to work for than Reitz. The only fault I had with him he did not pay as much as I would like to have had. As I cannot think of anything more to write I will close by asking you to write soon.

Yours truly,
John Rieley

Be sure to write soon. I wrote two letters home since Sept. 15th – did you get them?

John

94

Camp at Woodville, Ala.
November 17, 1863

Dear Mother and folks:

I sent herewith $40.00. We were paid a few days ago up to the 31ª of October. We have not done anything since I wrote last. We will probably stay here all Winter.

Please excuse this hasty letter. I have not heard anything from John for a long time.

Yours truly,

Frank Rieley

Knoxville, Dec. 6th, 1863

Dear Mother and Sister

I received your most welcome letter of Oct. 24th and was much pleased to hear from home again. I would have answered it before but we have been hemmed in by the rebels and could not send a letter home if I had wrote one. What will you think when I tell you that I have seen Frank. Maybe you will be surprised the same as I was when I saw him the other day for he came into camp when I thought he was 100 miles away. I suppose you have heard about Andrew Bishop getting wounded. He got a pretty close call this time but he is coming out all right again. He was here in camp talking with us Battery boys when Frank came in so we all met together and talked about old time and how we would make the copper heads get if we were home now. I will not give you much of an account of the time we had here with the rebs all around us for you will see it in the papers better than I can tell you. When the rebels first surrounded us there was only two days of rations in town for Burnsides Army and before they left we had to live on a half pound of meal a day and it was such a nice meal to – the took the corn and ground it up cob and all and gave it to us with ¾ pound of pork to get fat on. Well I did get fat on it for now I weigh 170 pounds, the most I have ever weighed. As it is getting dark I suppose I will have to stop writing. We expect to be paid off in a few days for four months that I don't know how I will send any home for there is no express here of any kind. I got them stamps you sent me and all the letters you wrote up to Oct 24th and Frank has one from home the 9th of November. Charlie Chessley was shot through the heart in the last fight at Chattenooga. Mich Molar was in the hospital and was not in the fight. The Neville boys are all well. When you get this letter you will have an answer to all I have received up to date. Write soon.

John Rieley

Knoxville, Dec. 15, 1863

Dear Mother

As I have a chance to send a letter by a man going over the mountains I thought I would write a few lines and send you a receipt for $40 dollars that I let the State Agent have.   You will have to draw it in Cleveland.   There is no news here of any importance. I wrote a letter about a week since and for fear that you did not get it I will tell you again that I saw Frank and he was well. As it will be about Christmas or New Years when you get this I will wish you all a Merry Christmas and a Happy New Year. I will now stop to write anymore.

John Rieley

Be sure to write soon.

Knoxville   Dec. 27th, 1863

Dear Mother

As I have a few spare moments I thought I would improve them by writing you a few lines to let you know that I am well. We are kept so busy at working Forts that I don't have much time to write. I wrote you a letter about two weeks since and sent a receipt for 40 dollars. Did you get it? The rebels are still about 25 or 30 miles from here but I don't know what they are doing half as well as I would if I was at home and read the papers every day. I think we will stay here all winter for we have turned over all our horses. We are now drawing quarter rations and if we did not buy one thing and another we would go pretty hungry some times. All we draw from the Government now is beef and black bread and not half as much as of that as I would like to eat but still I get along pretty well for I have got a peck of meal and three pounds of fresh pork that I bought and paid $1.40 for. Corn meal is worth $3.00 a bushel, flour $8.00 a hundred[33], coffee $1.50 a pound, beef 20 ¢ a pound and everything else in proportion. The time the rebels were around here our winter quarters were all torn down. Our Battery has been scattered all around town and when the rebels left here we got all together and commenced building winter quarters again and before we had them done our section of the Battery had to leave to go into a fort on the other side of and here the other day the rest of the boys had to leave to go into another fort so I think I will quit building winter quarters. I have read in history about soldiers going bare footed in the winter but I never saw it before. There is plenty of them bare footed here and I am pretty near to be the same myself. I have not heard of Frank since he left here. I think he went back to Chattanooga. I must stop writing for I have to go to work in a few minutes. You must write soon for I have not had a letter in about two months. Yours of Oct. 24th being the last I received. How does Willie like his new shop?

Yours truly,

John Rieley

---

[33] A term of weight measurement, equally approximately 100 pounds.

Dear Mother and Sister

I received your most welcome letter of Dec. 27th a few days since and was much pleased to hear from home again. I have a moment to write at this time. The smallpox is about as thick here as it is up there for we have one hospital here with 25 men in it with the smallpox. I would have written sooner but I have not felt well for a week or so. I have had a bad cold. I have not heard from Frank since I saw him here but I suppose he has re-enlisted and is on his way home or maybe he is home already for he told me (when I saw him) that he would re-enlist. I will send you one of the Brownlow's papers with this letter and it will give you and idea how things are going on in this part of rebeldom. You wanted to know that kind of time I had at Christmas, well I will tell you there was nothing going on throughout the day only feasting on our little half rations of corn meal and mule mean – no, I will take that back for it was not mule meat but it was worse – it was beef that was drove from Kentucky about 100 miles without anything to eat and when they go here they was not able to drive up to the front. Well I think I had better quit writing about grub or you will think I go hungry. You must not think so for I have not went hungry since I have been here. Well I must tell you about Christmas. Four of us boys thought it was too quiet for Christmas so we went to town and the first thing we saw was a lot of what we thought was a pile of rags but when we got close to them we found out it was a pack of deserters from Longstreet. We then heard some music up in a building and we went up and it was a nigger show but we had not Lincoln scrip[34] to spare so we did not go in but we saw a candle burning and we thought we would want it so when the door keep went in and shut the door one of the boys took it along. We went and the next we saw a wagon standing on the top of a big hill and we started it over and part of it went down the hill and part of it didn't. We then saw a big dog and a purp[35] and we threw some stones at it and started for camp and lit the candle and then talked about home until we got sleepy and then went to bed. That is all I remember about Christmas. The boys are all well and I can eat my half rations. Write soon.

John Rieley

---

[34] A slang term referring to the currency of the United States of America at the time.
[35] Most probably a hand-written mistake, referring to a young dog.

Knoxville,   Feb. 16ᵗʰ 1864

Dear Mother and Sister

As we are going to leave Knoxville in the morning, I thought I would write you a few lines before leaving. We had orders to leave this morning at 9 o'clock and report to Morristown which is 92 miles from there on the road to Richmond but we did not get ready soon enough and the train went off and left us this morning when we got orders to move. Each one of us had almost a wagon load of furniture and not a team in the Battery so the boys had to leave everything but what they could tote on their backs. After we were all ready we started for the depot which is about a mile from camp and as soon as we got there we had to turn around and come back to camp again. I will not write more this time for the boys are cutting up so that it is almost impossible to write. We have just been paid four months pay and that with the excitement of leaving in the morning makes the boys almost crazy. I suppose you got that money I sent home but you have not said anything about it yet. I will send some more home as soon as I have the chance. The boys are all well. Mich Miller and the Neville boys are all well.

John Rieley

Dear Mother

I received your most welcome letter of Jan. 6ᵗʰ a few days since and was much pleased to hear from home again. I don't see why it takes so long for your letters to get to me – it takes them always about a month to come through. I ton' thin you write as often as you ought for I have not received but two letters from home this year. I have not heard from Frank since I saw him here but I suppose he is at home before now for he told me that he would re-enlist and I saw by the papers that the 3ʳᵈ Ohio Cavalry had re-enlisted but I don't know how it will be with him for I heard that all the men that was home on furlough was ordered into the field again. I think that will be rough on the boys but if it will help to put down this rebellion I think they will come back cheerful. Our Battery is all together again. We are quartered in a large College. It is larger than the one on the Heights and it is on a large hill and we are building a large Fort around it. We are working on it everyday and expect to have it done in about three weeks. We get up in the morning at day-light to roll call then get breakfast and then go to work with our picks and shovels and work until noon then have one hour for dinner and work at one o'clock and work till sundown. We then get supper. We don't draw any candles so I don't have much to write. We have had some of the as good weather since January 1ˢᵗ as I ever saw or heard tell of. Some days it would be so warm that I would sweat in my shirt sleaves. You don't see any such weather in Ohio. At this season of the year. The smallpox is pretty plenty here yet. One of our boys has it, his name is Ed Morse. There was one of our boys died of it here in the hospital about a week since. His name was T. J. Poole, he has been sick ever since we came into Tennessee. We commenced to draw full rations again today which made the boys feel pretty well. William Hartzell has gone to Kentucky to take care of the Captain's horses. John Lowe is well and so are all the Burgh boys and I never felt better.

Yours truly,

John Rieley

Dear Mother:

I received your most welcome letter of Feb. 13th today and was much pleased to hear from home again and I also received yours of Jan 22nd a few days since and had no time to answer it until now, I wrote you a letter a week ago. Did you get it? I don't have much time to write yet for they keep us to work everyday. We have just come in from work and got our supper. This letter of yours came through pretty quick for once. I see you have got into your head that I am pretty hard up, well I was about two weeks ago but I have got a new suit of clothes now and feel tip-top. You would not believe how good it makes a soldier feel to get a new suit of clothes after he has been ragged as we were but now have new clothes and plenty to eat. I have not heard from Frank. I wish you would write as soon as you hear from him so I may know how he is getting along. There is nothing I would want from home unless it would be that tobacco that Reitz spoke of sending but he can't send it by express for there is nothing of that kind here. I have got a new pair of boots and they gave about one inch of leather sole on them. What would you think of them walking across your floor, do you think it would make much noise? Do you have any surprise parties there in Brooklyn this winter? I saw Mich Miller and Dick Neville the other day. John Neville was on duty so he could not come up but Dick said he was well. Dick and Mich looked first rate. They are in the 93rd O.V.I.[36] Company O. They said they could not see the re-enlist. I think I could not see it either if my time was near out as theirs. I have not heard how Morris is since I last wrote. He is in the hospital here with the small pox. The last time I heard from him he was getting better. All the boys you know in the Battery are well. If Mr. Reitz wants to send that tobacco he can send it by mail. Tell Mrs. Reitz I have got five pair of new socks so I will not want what she spoke of sending but I thank her just as much for her generous feeling as I would if I had got them. As I can't think of more to write, I will close by asking you to write soon. Give my best respects to Mr. and Mrs. Reitz and write soon.

Yours truly,

John Rieley

---

[36] Ohio Volunteer Infantry

Old Vet:

As I heard that you were at home I thought I would write you a few lines. If I had known where you were I would have wrote before. What did you want to be in such a hurry leaving here for? I went over the next morning to see you and get some of them flap-jacks but you were gone and I did now know where you went and never heard until yesterday when I got a letter from home that said you were at home. Well, Frank, I hope that you will have a good time while you are at home. Andrew Bishop started for home a few days since on furlough for thirty days but I suppose you will see him before this reaches you. I think I would like to be at home with you'ns and then you'ns and we'ns might have a pretty good old time but I think you will have it anyhow. I had an Ohio dinner today. We drew a lot of stuff from the Sanitary Commission[37] here in the grub line. Well I must tell you what I had for dinner. I had stewed apples, stewed grapes, sour kraut, good bread and butter, good tea such as you would get at home with sugar and milk in it and other things too numerous to mention. I think that is a pretty good dinner for a soldier, don't you? Mich Miller and Jack Neville are here in a camp close by. They are all well but they cold not see re-enlisting. I think that would be my fix if my time was near out as theirs. Frank, I want you to write and let me know what you have been doing since I saw you. Well Frank, you must let any of them Copperheads crowd you off the side walk for I think three fourths of it ought to belong to the soldiers. If you are around where there is plenty beer and plenty of men to treat – why just take a drink for me. Well I must bring this to a close. Write soon and tell me all the news. Tell Mary Ann that I received her letter of Feb. 27th. Hoping you may have a good time whilst you are at home I close.

John Rieley

Direct yours to – 19th Battery O.L.A.
            Knoxville, Tennessee

---

[37] The United States Sanitary Commission was a private relief agency created by federal legislation on June 18, 1861, to support sick and wounded soldiers of the U.S. Army during the American Civil War.

Dear Sister:

I received your most welcome letter of March 14th and was much pleased to hear from home again. I should have answered it sooner but the weather has been so cold (and nothing to shelter us from it but our dog tents) that it was almost impossible to write. I wrote you a letter the 16ht of this month did you get it. We left Knoxville on the 17th of this month and went to Morristown stayed there one night or almost one night for we were roused out of our beds about one o'clock in the morning and told that we had to march to Mossy Creek which is 16 miles from Morristown and 28 miles from Knoxville. Well we layed around until about 7 o'clock in the morning when we strapped our knapsacks on our backs and started. My knapsack was good deal of trouble at first for that was the first time I had lugged my knapsack on a march but before night it didn't bother me at all for my feet got so sore that I forgot that I had a knapsack strapped on me with two big blankets, four shirts, 5 pair of socks, an overcoat, one jacket, and a lot of small trinkets, a haversack full of grub, a canteen, and a coffee pot. What do you think of that load? Well we got here all safe and sound and have been here ever since. Since we have been here we have got a new Battery of four guns, they are 10 pound parrot guns which is the best kind of a gun that there is in the Army. I expect that we will have some running around to do this summer for our and another Battery is all that has got horses in this Department. We have had some pretty rough weather here. It commenced snowing and it didn't stop until there was about 12 inches of snow on the ground which was the most snow I have seen this winter but it did not stay on the ground long. It has been snowing pretty much all day but it melts as fast as it falls and forms into mud. I received a letter from Frank yesterday. I will send receipt home in this letter for 40 dollars on the County Treasury. Write soon and let me know when you get it. I would like to have been there. Give my best respects to all and write soon.

John Rieley

---

[38] The location of a minor battle of the American Civil War, occurring on December 29, 1863, in Jefferson County, Tennessee.

Dear Mother and Sister:

I received your welcome letter of March 25ᵗʰ and was much pleased to hear from home again. You spoke about us being glad to leave Knoxville well I for one would as soon stay there until my time was out as to be on the move. I am not so fast for moving now as when I first entered the Army. Let a man go through the hardships that the men in this Army did in coming over the mountains from Kentucky and he will want to lay in camp for a while I think. I had a nice thing for last month that I was in Knoxville. There was ten men detailed out of our Battery to oversee a lot of darkies that was at work on the Fort. Well I was one of them and John Low was along – the only one that you know. Well we got a new tent an a lot of cooking utensils and was living old gat when the Battery got orders to move. If we had stayed there we would have had an all summer job. All we had to do was stand around and keep the darkies to work the rest of the boys that stated with the Battery had to work with their shovels and picks every day. You asked if we had got the Forts done that we were at work on. Well we didn't and I don't believe any of them will be done until this war is over. I believe you asked me in one of your letters how Morse was. I am very sorry to tell you that he is dead, he died the 26th of Feb. and he was dead 3 or 4 days before anyone in the Battery knew anything about it. He was as good a boy as there is in the Battery. I wrote you a letter about a week since and sent an order in it for forty dollars on the State or County Treasury and wish you would write and let me know if you received it or not. There is no word here of any importance. I suppose we will stay here until we get some new horses for the ones we have now are about played out and some of them has been in the service three years and over. We have got some four or five horses that has been in the army of the Potomac and at the siege of Vicksburgh and also in the siege of Knoxville and are pretty good horses yet. I suppose Frank has left home before this. I would liked first rate to have been at home with him but it is impossible. The boys in the Battery are all well and I never felt better. Direct your letters to Knoxville until I tell you different. I must close by asking you to write soon. John Bissell went a letter to your box. I told him to do it for it would be safe for he sent an order in it for some money. In haste.

John Rieley

The following is a transcript of a conversation with Frank Rieley about what occurred since his previous letter of November 17, 1863 as there were no letters that had been saved until mid-April, 1864.

April 18, 1864

Shortly after this letter (5 days) the battle of Chattanooga was fought. The 3rd OVC was guarding roads across from Chattanooga during that battle of November 22 – 27. Immediately after that battle they were sent by Gen. Grant to escort Col. J. H. Wilson of his staff with a message to Knoxville to General Burnside advising him of the relief being sent to him as Gen. Longstreet was besieging him there.

The found Burnside in better shape than supposed to be and father visited his brother and schoolmates in that regiment 41st O. In travelling to Knoxville, they went through Athens, Tenn. and London, Tenn. and had numerous skirmishes on the way.

Co. I3 OVC was later sent to Cumberland Gap on guard duty at the pass through the Winter. He was allowed to go home on a furlough later in the Winter.

Camp near Columbia, Tenn.
April 18, 1864

Dear Mother:

It is now nearly three weeks since I left home and I have not had a letter from you yet. I wrote one to you as soon as I reached the regiment which was two weeks ago but suppose your answer has miscarried.

I reached the regiment on Sunday April 3rd which was then at Nashville. Nothing was said to be by the officers because I staid over my furlough time. We staid in Nashville until the 13th of April when we left for this place. We did not have horses and therefore we had to foot it which we didn't like very much. We reached Columbia on the 16ht of April, tired and footsore. The distance is forty miles. We are doing garrison duty her having relieved a lot of cavalry who were mounted and ordered to the front.

I received a letter from brother John about a week ago. He was with the battery (19th O) at Masfy Creek about twelve miles above Knoxville.

I sent home a receipt for that overcoat and the other things of mine which are at the American Express office in Cleveland. If you did not get them, I wish that you would write and let me know in your next letter.

According to appearances, we will not be wanted until the middle of the Summer and will be left here to guard the railroad, but I was mistaken about being left in Nashville and I may be mistaken this time. I have been detailed as sergeant of the Provost guard in the regiment and now I have easy times hardly anything to do. No drill guard or picket duty to trouble myself with. In fact time is a little too plenty to be healthy and therefore I wish you would write often as I have plenty of time to answer all your letters.

While I was at Nashville, I went to town and saw John Driver who used to work with me a Lowman's. He is now working in Nashville making wagons for the government.

Direct your next to Frank Rieley, Provost Guard 3 O V V C[39], Columbia, Tenn.

Love to all the family,

Frank Rieley

---

[39] Ohio Veteran Volunteer Cavalry

Camp near Columbia, Tenn.
April 22, 1864

Dear Mother and Sister:

I received your welcome letter of the 13th this morning and was much pleased to heart that you were all well. It was long in coming so that I began to fear that you were sick and some trouble had prevented you from writing. I am glad to hear that you received those things of mine for I feared that you would not get them.

We left Nashville on the 13th and marched to this place by foot which we reached on April 16th. We are doing garrison duty here having relieved a lot of cavalry who had horses. We received part of our carbines and sabres but not enough to arm all of our regiment. We do not know when we will get horses but I guess not for at least a month to come. As soon as we get horses, we will be sent to the front for they need cavalry very much there. The 4th O. V V C is also here without horses, an the 1st O V C[40] is at Nashville also without horses. The 10th OVC is at Ringold, Ga. And I think they will have something to do this Summer which will not be as much to their liking as charding on Dutch Groceries. I have been detailed Sergeant of the Provost Guard which is a much easier position than in the Company. I now have no drill, picket or guard duty to do. The Provost Guard is made up of a Lieut., one sergeant, one corporal and ten privates, one out of each Company of the regiment. The duty is to march in the rear of the regiment and pick up all stragglers and take charge of prisoners until they can be disposed of. While in camp all we have to do is lay in our tents and if we hear anyone fire a gun or a pistol, go and arrest him.

Direct your letters to Frank Rieley, P.G. OVC Columbia, Tenn.

I received a letter from John two weeks ago. The weather is very fine here, warm days and cool nights. Trees are budding and blossoming and Spring is with us again.

Don't be afraid to write often for fear that I will not have time to answer your letters. I have plenty of time and to spare. Give my love to all the family.

Yours truly,

Frank Rieley

---

[40] Ohio Volunteer Cavalry

Dear Mother and Sister

I received your kind letter of the 25th and was much pleased to hear from home and to hear that you was well. We have moved our camp since I last wrote home. We are now about 4 miles from Lexington in a very nice camp in the woods. The trees are all green they are bout as far ahead as they will be in the last part of May around home. The weather is very pleasant it is warm enough for us to lay in the shade of the trees in the day time but it is pretty cold nights. Captain Shields is with us again and the boys were glad when he came. Adam is in town and he will be with us again in a few days. I have not heard from Frank for some time and I was glad to hear he was well. I don't agree with him in thinking the war will be over next fall. When the rebels are drove out of Vicksburg then I will talk about the war coming to a close. I think if it was not for them copperheads and butternuts up North the war would be over now. In two weeks after this war is over and the soldiers get home there won't be a live copperhead or butternut in the United States. I would sooner kill one of them than Jeff Davis[41]. Who told you that all the stuff in that box was spoiled. All my things (except the paper and I can use all of it) are just as good as when it left home. The sheet of paper is one of the worst. I am glad to hear that you like that register so well. It cost one dollar. Since I commenced writing I heard that Adam has gone to Cincinnati to the hospital. It is thought he will get his discharge. As I can't think of any more to write I will close by asking you to write soon.

John Rieley

---

[41] Jefferson Davis, the President of the Confederate States of America

Dear Mother:

I now seat myself to answer your letter of April 12th which I had ought to done nearly two weeks since but I have been pretty busy during that time for we have marched about 112 miles. We stopped at Knoxville a few days and left our four parrot guns there and got four of our old ones and some new horses and started for this place where we arrived the night before last. This is the same place where Frank camped two months last winter. I will not write a very long letter this time. We are going to move again in the morning but I don't know what way we are going this time but I think it will be towards Dalton. This place is just 40 miles from there. While we were at Knoxville we got four barrels of sour kraut and four barrels of potatoes from Sanitary Commission so we lived pretty well for a few days. I think that Sanitary Commission has got to be a pretty good thing. I received them things that you sent with Andrew Bishop. He got a pass and came up to Mossy Creek while we were laying there. The boys are all well and so am I. I will not write you any more this time for I have to fix up some for the march tomorrow.

Yours truly,

John Rieley

P.S. Direct your letters to the 19th Battery O.L.A.[42]., 2nd Division 23rd Army Corps, Charleston, Tenn.

John Rieley

---

[42] Ohio Light Artillery

Dear Mother and Sister

I received you kind letter of May 1st today and I was much pleased to hear from home. I also received your letter of April 25th and answered it. The men that got hurt are quite well now. Readhead has to keep his hand tied up in a sling but he is around the camp every day. The other two boys are on duty again. We have left Camp Shield in the woods about 4 miles from town. It was a good camp and I would just as leave stay there as any other place until the war is over. You say you wish I was there to go to that party. Well I wish I was there to break it up. I have not forgotten about that insult yet and I don't think I will very soon. I think if I was at home Maggie wouldn't bring a party to our house. I don't see how she can get down so low as to bring one there any how. I got the stamps you sent me and should have spoken about it before but I had forgotten about it. You asked me in your last letter if we have been singing here the same as we did in Camp Cleveland. Well we have singing about every other night. We get the daily papers here so we keep pretty well posted about war matters. There are eleven of us in a tent and we all take turns at paying of a paper. I wish you would send me the directions to Frank. I wrote him two letters and I have not had an answer yet. The 2nd Ohio Cavalry went through here about three weeks ago. I saw Andrew Bishop and he looked first rate. We was mustered in for pay last Thursday but I suppose it will stay here until the war is over. I don't see a fight. The Battery is first rate health now. There is not a man on the sick list but Readhead. We had a heavy thunderstorm last night. I cannot think of anything more to write so I will close. Give my love to all.

John Rieley

Camp near Columbia, Tenn.
May 6, 1864

Dear Mother:

I received your letter of April 28ᵗʰ yesterday and glad to hear that you are all well. Times are very dull here at present and they are apt to remain so until we move from this place.

Part of our regiment has gone to Nashville for horses for the regiment and expect to be back with them in about two weeks. As soon as we receive the horses, times will not be so dull for I expect that we will be sent to the front as soon as we are mounted and things will be lively enough then according to present appearances. Well I don't care if we can only whip out the rebels this Summer, how lively the times are. I also think that if we do not whip them this Summer, we will never do so. That order calling out the militia or home guards suits old soldiers pretty well. It looks as fi the government was at last waking up and meant to do something this Summer.

How do the Graham family like it and all the rest of the stay at homes. Have they all got the "rumatism" and "sore toes"? HI hope that they will get a taste of active service they will remember for a while. Let me know about the battery (Wright Graham & Co.'s) in your next.

We expect to be paid in a day or two for three months and if we are I will send some money home by express to J.B. Smith.

Tell Miss Brainard that I wrote her a letter about three weeks ago. If she did not get it, it is not my fault.

The weather here is pleasant here now. Bright Spring sunshine, flowers, birds, etc. without end. I will try and get them photo's taken here if I can. I am very sorry to hear of so much sickness at home, but I suppose it can not be helped.

Our regiment is very healthy, scarcely any sickness. Don't you think the draft and the ordering out of the militia caused a great deal of sickness in our neighborhood. Well as I cannot think of any more nonsense I will stop for the present.

Give my love to all the family.

Yours as ever,

Frank Rieley

Lexington   May 15ᵗʰ

Dear Sister

I received your most welcome letter of May 10ᵗʰ soon after date and was much pleased to hear from home. I had a letter from Frank yesterday, he was well. He have been fixing up for a review for two or three days. It came off yesterday. We had our guns polished up as bright as a new dollar and our harness greased and we had our company go to meeting clothes on. Captain got us some blackening and we all polished our boot so we looked old gay. We was reviewed by General Wilcox. We live old high here. Now we have ham, soft bread, potatoes, pancakes etc. We had a dance here last night but the worst trouble was we had no girls. There was some big bettering going on in camp last Sunday about Richmond and talk was that we was going home pretty soon but if you had come into camp the next day you have seen some long faces and heard some big swearing. How is the Sunday School getting along there now. I have some washing to do and there is not much to write so I will have to write a short letter. I suppose you know that every one has to do his own washing in the army. The Burgh boys are all well and I have never felt better. Give my best wishes to all.

                                                John Rieley

Camp near Columbia, Tenn.
May 15, 1864

Dear Mother:

We were paid off yesterday and as the Ohio State Agent was here I thought that that would be the best way to send money home. Enclosed you will find a check on the Country Treasury for $75.00.

I expect we will leave this place in a few days, as we have received our horses and be sent to the front. Everything is dreadfully dull except the excitement of the news from Virginia. The train from Nashville comes in about 11:00 A.M. and then there is a great rush for newspapers. Those who are lucky enough to get papers are soon surrounded by a crowd of eager listeners who stand with open mouths trying to catch each word as it is read. Then if some great deed is recorded about taking prisoners or cannon, the crowd commences shouting "Bully for Grant". The war will soon be over, etc.

I will write again before we leave this place if I get a chance. Write soon and send some postage stamps.

Yours truly,

Frank Rieley

Georgia

Camp near Cassville,

May 22ʳᵈ, 1864

Dear Mother and Sister:

I received your most welcome letter of May 9ᵗʰ a few days ago and was much pleased to hear from home again. Since I last wrote home we have had some pretty hard time of it. Yesterday and today we have been resting and it is the first time we have been in a camp only to stop over night (and a great many of the nights we were in line of battle or on the move) since I last wrote home. We have been in two fights and they were pretty hard one too. I suppose you will see by the papers that the 23ʳᵈ Corps was in the fight and our Division done the hardest fighting that was done. There was no one in the Battery got a scratch but me and I was more scared than hurt. There was a shell exploded over my head and a small piece of it struck me on the left ear which just started the blood. We had two horses killed, a solid shot through one of their necks and the other one was struck with a piece of shell on the rump and it took a chunk of flesh out of him that would weigh 10 pounds. We are going to lay here until morning and then we are going on a twenty days march but I don't know where we are going any more than it is some place where there is some rebels. I have been pretty sick for the last few days. I have had the disentary⁴³ but I feel better now than I have for the last two months. I suppose you will not get another letter from me for the next 20 days but if I have a chance to write on the march I will do it. You must write as often as you can and the letters will follow the Battery no matter where it goes. I have not heard from Frank in some time only what you have written but there is a good reason for I have not answered his last letter yet. I saw a man today that left Columbia, Tenn. 4 or 5 days ago and he said that the 3ʳᵈ Ohio Cavalry had started for this Army but I think they are around on the right flank. I must close and write a few lines to Frank. Write soon and direct to 2ⁿᵈ Division, 23ʳᵈ Corps, Chattanooga.

John Rieley

How is Dan Graham coming along.

---

[43] A mis-spelling of Dysentery, an inflammatory disorder of the intestine.

Camp near Big Shanty Station, Ga.
June 14, 1864

Dear Mother:

I received two letters from you some time back and was glad to hear from home. I have not the time now to write all the particulars of our march from Columbia to this place, as the mail leaves in a few minutes and I want to send this as I will not get another chance very soon to send a letter.

I saw Dick Neville. He was well. I suppose I will have a chance to see John as he is with this army, although I do not know at what point. We have had several fights since we left Columbia, one at Courtland, Ala, and another at Moulton, Ala. And one at this place. We came out best in the first two, which we had with five regiments of cavalry and one battery. We had three regiments and two pieces of artillery – 1ˢᵗ, 3ʳᵈ and 4ᵗʰ Ohio. We joined this army about a week ago. Three days ago, our regiment was sent on a reconnaissance toward the rebel lines and went a little too far. We ran into a whole division of rebel cavalry. They drove us back with a loss of twelve men wounded and one taken prisoner. We are now laying within sight of the rebels but they do not trouble us very much. They are evidently waiting for us to attack them and I suppose they won't have long to wait.

I will write again as soon as we get settled down a little. I expect we will have lively times until Atlanta is taken. We are now within twenty five miles of Atlanta. Don't be alarmed if you do not hear from us very soon as I expect this is the last chance I will have to write for a couple of weeks.

Excuse mistakes as I have written this on the double quick. Give my love to all the family. Direct your next c/o of Lieut. E. Haines, 3 O V C Kingston, Ga.

Yours truly,

Frank Rieley

Nashville, July 6, 1864

Dear Mother:

I suppose you will begin to think I am gone up or something for it is a good while since you heard from me. Since I last wrote home I have been pretty sick. I have not felt well since we left Mossy Creek but the last month is what knocked me in the head. I have had the remittent fever and it has just taken the flush off of me. I would have written before this but I was not able. My fever was broke about 5 or 6 days since but I am very weak yet. I have got so poor that you would know me if you saw me. I will not write but a few lines this time for I didn't feel able but I hope I will soon be strong enough to write a letter every week. I am pretty hard up for money and I would send home for some but I don't know what minute I will be ordered away from here but as soon as I find out if I am going to stay here I will send for some. You must write as soon as you can for I may leave and I want to hear from home the worst kind. I have not heard from home in 6 weeks but I think there is some letters at the Battery for me. Direct yours to Cumberland Hospital[44], 1st Division.

John Rieley

---

[44] A Civil War hospital in Nashville, Tennessee

Nashville, July 25, 1864

Dear Mother and Sister

It is now over two months since I have heard from home so I wish you would write as soon as you receive this for I am very anxious to hear from home and I wish you would send me a few dollars for it will be some time before I get any from Uncle Sam as I am not with the Battery and I know that I will not get any here for they have paid off all hands and the cook. I wish you would let me know how and where Frank is for it is some time since I have heard from him I have not had a letter from him since he left home. There is no news here to write and nothing to see only sick and wounded soldiers. One hospital is outside of town. We have large tents and are very comfortable. If you don't get this before the 31" you need not write for I expect to leave here for the Battery in about two weeks. I am getting along first rate and can eat rations up clean. Write soon and direct to John Rieley 1" Division, Cumberland Hospital, Nashville, Tenn.

John Rieley

Cincinnati, July 27, '64

Dear Mother:

I received your two letters this morning and was much pleased to hear from home. We have just been paid off and I have about five minutes to write before we start for Lexington. I will send 20 dollars in this letter. The boys are all well and so am I. Direct your next to Lexington. I wrote a letter home a few days ago. Did you get it? Give my love to all.

John Rieley

Camp near Atlanta, Ga.
August 2, 1864

Dear Mother:

I have just received a letter from Mr. and Mrs. Alfred Tilton, informing me that they were married which surprised me somewhat although I expected something of the kind, but I didn't think it would come off so soon. I know your opinion of the match and therefore I need not ask any questions. I hope you will not fret yourself to death over it. You are not to blame and if anyone suffers, she will be the principle one to suffer and have no one to blame but herself. She chose for herself and I would give myself no more trouble on their account. I hope you will not work yourself sick. If you have a great deal of work to do, you had better get a girl to live with you and if you need money do not hesitate to use what little I have at home. I can get along very well without it. I don't need money in the army and if I get our of the army safe and sound, it will be an easy matter to get along.

I am glad to hear that John is getting better. I was over to the 19th battery last week. All the boys were well. I also heard from the Neville boys at the same time. They are both well. We are kept very busy now making raids on the rebel railroads. We have been on two raids since we crossed the Chattahootchie River.

I am in good health – never was in better than at present. The weather is not and disagreeable. If you find the number of the hospital that John is in, let me know and I will write him.

I would write a longer letter if I had time, but we are just about to move and I can't finish this letter.

Write soon and direct to

Frank Rieley, Co.I 3rd OVC
Nearnetta, Ga.

Dear Mother and Sister

I received your most welcome letter of Aug 4th soon after date and was much pleased to hear from home again and to hear that you are all well. I am well at present and so are all of the Brooklyn Boys. We left Cincinnati soon after I last wrote to you. We crossed the river to Covington and loaded on the cars. It was about dark when we left there. We travelled all night in a heavy rain and when we got into camp here we were all pretty well tired out. You might have seen us laying around under trees or where ever we could get out from under the hot sun. Since we started on the chase after Morgan we have traveled about 1,000 miles most of the time by rail road and nearly every time we moved it was to go all night. The boys got so sleepy that if we stopped 5 minutes on the road they would nearly all be strung along some fence fast asleep. We had 4 men desert us while in Ohio. Their names are E.W. Davis, J.A. Goode, P.H. Galegar, G. Grosley. The Captain says he has got their names in the Cleveland papers as deserters. I have just got a letter from Frank. There is some talk of us all going home this winter on discharge furloughs. Some of the boys were asking Captain for a furlough and he told them that all the heavy artillery in this state was going home on discharge furloughs this winter. We leave here in the morning for Hickmans Bridge which is 20 miles from here. We start at 4 o'clock. The boys all hate to leave there for Lexington seems like a home to most of us. You spoke of us having to fall back on Uncle Sam's grub, well we have not fell back on it yet but we will have to as soon as we got to Hickman's Bridge. Since we came to Lexington we have had onions, fresh and corned beef that we could stuff down our throat. We have plenty of milk too. I had like to forgotten the milk. John Bissell has just come in with a water pail full. He has been milking some of the neighbors cows. Who was elected in our neighbourhood for school director last spring? How is Willie getting along in the shop? Give my best wishes to Mr. and Mrs. Reitz, my love to the family and then write to me.

John Rieley

Camp near Atlanta, Ga.
August 24, 1864

Dear Mother:

I received your welcome letter of August 11* yesterday and was much pleased to hear from home again. We have just returned from a raid on the Atlanta and Macon Railroad. I will not trouble you with an account of the expedition because you will get all the details from the newspaper. We were under the command of Gen. Kilpatrick. We cut the railroad at a place called Jonesboro, destroyed four or five miles of track. We proceeded down the railroad about four miles and rain into a large infantry force (rebel). We attacked them and found that they had more men than we had. We fought them ferociously when they attacked us on the rear. They had us surrounded and there was only one way out that was to charge through their lines. We did charge them and they opened a battery on us but could not stop the charge. We captured the rebel battery but could not get all of it off the field. We succeeded in getting one piece away with us. We lost a great many men. Our regiment lost forty five men in the raid mostly wounded only three or four taken prisoners. Our dead and part of our wounded were left in the hands of the enemy. Our whole loss will be five hundred. Co. I. did not lose a man. Our regiment did the hardest of the fighting. We were armed with seven shooters and we laid out three or four hundred of the rebels at least. The 10* OVC were with us and lost a great many men. I saw John Holler after the fight and he came through all right. Col. Eli Long commanding our brigade was wounded.

I will not write any more about the raid because I expect you will see it in the Cleveland papers. Do not take it so hard about sister Mary getting married, but let her go. If anyone suffers it will be herself that suffers most. If you need any help you had better get a girl to live with you and if you want money, do not hesitate about using what little I have at home.

Yours as ever,

Frank Rieley

Chatanooga, Sept. 6th, 1864

Dear Mother:

I guess you will begin to think that I have stopped writing or have forgotten you all together but it no so for there is not a day but what I think about home and after one year more of hard soldiering I will begin to think of seeing that dear old place HOME. Perhaps you will think I am getting home sick but it is no so far. I never was more contented in my life. I have been here now very near three weeks and expecting every day to leave for the Battery but I could not get a chance to go and I don't know how long it will be before I can. I would have written home before but I thought I would get to the Battery and write more from there so as that I could get a letter from home for I cannot get any while running around the way I have been since I left the Battery for I have never been in one place more than one or two days at a time. I am now in kind of a Convallescent Camp and have plenty to eat and not much work to do. Since I have been there I have seen Jim Knox and Philip Dratz. They are out now towards Nashville on a scout after Wheeler. I wrote a letter home from Nashville before I left there and you got it and answered it. I left word at the Hospital for them to send my letter on but I have not got any yet. Have you heard from Frank yet? As I cannot think of anything more to write I will bring this to a close.

John Rieley

Direct yours to John Rieley, 1st Battalion of Detatchment⁴⁵, Chattanooga, Tenn.

Hoping to hear from you soon I close..

John Rieley

---

45 A detachment is when you take a part of your "unit" whether it is a squad or company and send them to another "unit.

Camp near Cross Keys, Ga.
September 16, 1864

Dear Mother:

I received your welcome letter of September 5ᵗʰ a few days ago and was very glad to hear from home again. Since writing my last letter General Sherman has worked the rebels out of Atlanta. Our regiment has not been engaged in any fighting since the raid. We however were with the army when they made the flank movement to the southwest of Atlanta and went as far as Jonesboro. The 14ᵗʰ Corps had a pretty severe fight and thrashed the rebels soundly. That was on the 1ˢᵗ of September. On the 4ᵗʰ, we started back to Atlanta not because we could go no further, but because Gen. Sherman thought that his boys wanted rest after their hard campaign from Chattanooga to Atlanta. The 23ʳᵈ Corps is now at Decatur six miles out of Atlanta. I went over to the 19ᵗʰ Batter when they were on the march from Jonesboro to Decatur, and saw the boys but John (brother) was not with them. We went into camp at Decatur. The next day I was agreeably surprised to see John walking over to our regiment to see me. He had just come from Chattanooga to join his battery. He was looking somewhat poorly after his sickness in the hospital at Chattanooga, but he was gaining fast. The next day we left Decatur and came to this place that is thirteen miles from Atlanta and eight miles from Decatur. I expect the 19ᵗʰ Battery (John's regiment) are still at Decatur. We will probably lay here three or four weeks and then go for Macon, Ga.

I think the prospects are very good now for the closing of the war in six or seven months and in three months we can whip the rebels in that time if the northern rebels will keep quiet.

Direct your next to Atlanta, Ga.

If you could send me a few envelopes as I cannot get them here.

Yours as ever,

Frank Rieley

Dear Mother:

I received your letter of Sept. 16ᵗʰ a few days since and was much pleased to hear from home again and to hear that you were all well. I am as well as could be expected and improving every day. I left Chattanooga the 7ᵗʰ of Sept. and got to the Battery the next day and the boys were all glad to see me again. They did not expect to see me for they had heard that I had died in Chattanooga but I am worth 5 or 6 dead men yet I think. I have seen Frank two times when first I came here but the Cavalry all went away and do not know where he is. He looked first rate when I saw him. The boys here in the Battery have had a pretty rough time of it while I was sick. They had 8 men – one killed and 7 wounded and since died. A.B. Beaters wounded slight – E. Fairchild wounded – J. B. Hower slight – Martin Leonard thumb shot off – Henry Curtis hand partly shot off – Burrows slight in the arm. Since I came here we have turned over our guns, they being worn out. We have not got any new ones yet but we expect them before long. We were paid off a few days ago and I sent 75 dollars home with Captain Shields and told him to leave it with B. R. Beavis. John Bissell also sent 75 dollars to be left at the same place for his folks. I don't know as it was a very safe way to send it home but it the best I could do. Captain Shields is to leave it with Beavis house some night and tell him where it is from and suppose you had better go over to Beavis house some night and get it. John Bissell wrote a letter home a day or two since and I told him I would write in a day or two and speak about this so as to make a sure thing of it. If one or the other letters did no go through safe. So you better let his folks know if they have not already told you. Captain Shields has resigned on account of poor health in his family. The boys was very sorry to see him go. I got the letter you wrote to Nashville. I have not had any letter from Mary Ann yet. Write soon and let me know if you get that money. I am glad that Sylvester⁴⁶ has not forgotten me yet.

John Rieley

---

[46] John and Frank's sibling, Edwin Sylvester Rieley.

Gaylesville, Ala.
October 27, 1864

Dear Mother:

I received your kind letter of September 29th a week or so ago, but could not answer it before because the railroad was torn up between Atlanta and Chattanooga. I have not time to give you an account of all we went through since my last letter, because the mail will go out in one half hour and I want this letter to go with it.

We left Atlanta October 1st and have been on the march ever since. The rebel army have been making a raid on the railroad or in other words have been trying to starve our army out of Atlanta and the 4th, 14th, 15th, 17th and 23rd Corps of infantry and all the cavalry were sent after them but we have not succeeded in getting a fight out of them yet. Our division has had considerable skirmishing with them however. About two weeks ago our division captured two pieces of artillery and one hundred fifty prisoners from the rebels near Rome, Georgia. About the 12th of the month, we skirmished with them almost every day sine we left Atlanta. Our Company had had one man killed, Serg. Hoffinire, and Segt. Saltzgaber wounded. I saw John and Dick Neville near Marietta, Ga. about two weeks ago. They were with the regiment but expected to be mustered out of the service in a day or two. I saw the 23rd Corps but the 19th Battery was not with them. They stayed in Atlanta. Our division is out on a scout, but I was left back because I had no horse to ride.

Galesville is about twenty miles west of Rome, Ga. But I must close,

Direct your next to Rome, Ga.

Frank Rieley

Dear Mother and Sister:

As I have a little time I thought I would write a few lines to you. We are in the same place as we were the last time I wrote. There is no news of any account. We expect to stay here a month or so yet there is some talk of us going back to Covington but I don't think we will. There are six Batteries here with us. I wrote to Frank yesterday. I have not heard from him yet. If you have send me word how he is and where he is. Tell him to write to me when you write to him again. Send word how the Neville boys re getting along and where they are. We was roused out of a sound sleep the other night by the sound of a bugle and the orderly coming into our tents shouting the rebels was onto us. We all turned out and hitched up the horses as fast as we could. When they was all hitched up the Captain told us to unhitch that it was only to try us. It was only fifteen minutes from the time the bugle sounded until the harness was off from the horses. It was called quick time. The boys and myself are all well. I must stop writing as I cannot think of anything more to write. Give my love to all and write soon. Direct the same as in my letter of the first.

John

Louisville, Ky.
November 16, 1864

Dear Mother:

I expect that you will be surprised to learn that we are at Louisville, Ky. I wrote you in October but have not had an answer. We were then near Galesville, Ala. Soon after we moved to Rome, Ga. and turned our horses over to Gen. Kilpatrick's division which started south to join Sherman who has started an expedition down through Georgia. Our whole division was dismounted. We walked from Rome, Ga. to Calhoun where we took cars for Chattanooga. We laid at Chattanooga five or six days and held an election in our regiment, with the following results. Lincoln 330, McClellan 17[47]. Whilst in Chattanooga, I heard that the 19th Battery was there. I started to find them and found brother John and all the boys all well. The 19th was on the way to Nashville to get a new battery and fresh horses. They got on the cars the same day at Chattanooga that we did since then I have not seen them but I suppose they are at Nashville. We laid in Nashville a day and then got on the cars and came to this place. We will get horses in a few days and then I suppose we will start south again. I wish that if not too much trouble, you would send my overcoat through to me by express. I need an overcoat this Winter and if I draw one it will cost eleven dollars and the old one will do just as well, if I had it here. You can get a small box and pack it in it and if you want to send anything else such as a can of fruit packed in with the coat, I do not think it will cost more than three dollars to send it through. If it does you need not send it.

Brother Willie[48] can take it to the express office and ship it. If you send it, sent a letter by mail and let me know by what express you sent it. Send as soon a possible because we do not know how soon we may have to leave here.

Love,   Yours, etc.

F. Rieley

---

[47] An election that was held by the members of the Regiment after the National election, in which Lincoln ran as the Republican nominee against Democratic candidate George B. McClellan, who ran as the "peace candidate" without personally believing in his party's platform. In the real election on November 8, Lincoln won by over 400,000 popular votes on the strength of the soldier vote and following battlefield successes at Atlanta.[3] Lincoln was the first president to be re-elected since Andrew Jackson in 1832.

[48] Another sibling of Frank and John Rieley, William Lloyd Rieley.

Nashville, Nov. 24, 1864

Dear Mother:

I suppose you will think that I am getting pretty lazy for not writing sooner and I suppose you would be about right for I don't know what other excuse to make for not writing sooner. I commenced to write this letter 4 or 5 days ago but could not finish as I had to go after horses and since then the weather has been so cold that I could not write. Since I commenced this I received a letter from home written Nov. 2ⁿᵈ and one from Mary Ann written last July when I was in the hospital. The last letter I wrote home we were in Decatur, Ga. After we left there we went to Atlanta and build winter quarters three times. As soon as we would get fixed up for good and comfortable we would be ordered to move. We left Atlanta the 4ᵗʰ of this month and came to Chattanooga. We stayed there about one week and then came up here and since we have come here we have drew new horses and 4 new guns so I think we will soon be after the rebs again. I saw Frank when I was in Chattanooga. He looked first rate. I think he is here in Nashville now for they left Chattanooga the same night we did and he told me that they were coming here to draw new horses. They had no horses when I saw him. I heard about a week ago that you had got the money I sent home. John Bissell got a letter from his father and it did not take it as long to come through as it did mine. We have had some pretty cold weather here for the last few days but I have got good clothes, blankets and boots so I don't mind it so much as I did last winter in Knoxville. There is some talk of us going back there when we leave here but I can't whether we will or not. I hope not any how. One of our boys that was home on a furlough came back to the Battery yesterday and he says it is reported around there that I am dead but if any of them askes you about it tell that it aint so at least I don't think so. We are getting first rate grub since we came here. We have plenty of saur kraut, onions, potatoes, pork, beef, soft bread, coffee, sugar and so forth. The saur kraut, onions and potatoes are from Sanitary. If they would let me stay here about one month I would get as fat as a hog. Write soon and I will try to do better the next time my self.

John Rieley

Camp near Louisville
December 5, 1864

Dear Mother:

I received your letter of November 29th, 1864 and also the one of November 26th and was much pleased to hear from home once more. I have also received the box you sent me containing my overcoat, for which I am very thankful. I have nothing of any importance to write. We have not got our horses yet but will get them sometime next week, I guess and then will start for the front again. Times are very dull for us know and are getting photographs taken and I am going to send some of them home and I want you to put them out of the way until I want them again. I have not had any taken yet, but I will have some taken before I leave here. I cannot think of anything more to write at present and therefore I will stop.

Give my love to all the family and my thanks to Mrs. Howlett for that can of grapes.

Yours etc.

F. Rieley

Dear Mother and Sister"

I received your letter of *(illegible)* today and was very glad to hear from home. We have moved since last I wrote you but not very far. We moved closer to Lexington for a more convenient camp. The camp is named after a young girl that was going to school. Her brother had the Stars and Stripes over his house when Morgan came into town and Morgan took them down and the girl got a revolver and went to him and told him to deliver it up or she would blow his brains out. Morgan handed it over. I had a letter from Frank yesterday. He was well and at Nashville. I think we will stay here all winter. I had a letter from home a little over a week ago with the stamps and I wrote one just a week ago, have you got it? There has been a great many letters sent to boys in the Battery which they have not received. If Mr. Bissell comes down I wish you would go to Padocs hat store and get me a military cap size 7-1/8th and send me a pair of cotton gloves and my vest. If you get a cap ask for one the same as the 19th Battery got there. The price of them is one dollar. The boys re all well – all of them that you know. The weather is pretty cold here but we are quite comfortable. We have a stove in our tent and plenty of wood. There are two hospitals in Lexington but I don't know how the sick get along there for I have never been in any of them. As news is more scarce here than at home I will have to bring this to a close. Give my love to all the family and all enquiring friends.

Yours in much haste,

John

P.S. We expect to be paid in a few days.

December 14, 1864
Louisville, Ky.

Dear Mother:

We are still at Louisville but we have now got our horses and I think will soon leave for the front. I wrote a letter about a week ago. Have you received it. I then sent some photographs of some of the boys in our Company. I will send some of my own with this in another envelope. I have nothing very interesting to write and therefore I will stop.

F. Rieley

Louisville, Ky.
December 22⁰ᵈ 1864

Dear Mother:

I received your letter of the 18ᵗʰ today and was much pleased to hear from home once more.

The weather is very cold and severe at present, snow having fallen tow or three inches deep at present. I have sent eighteen photos already, have you received them all? I have also sent a soldier's memorial containing the names of the men in our Company.

We have received marching orders and will march next Saturday morning to what point I do not know, but suppose we will go to Nashville or down in Tennessee somewhere. We soldiers feel very god over the news from Gen. Thomas and the boys under him. I don't suppose I will have a chance to write again for some time but I will write as soon as I have a chance, as I have nothing interesting to write, I will close.

Frank Rieley

Dear Mother:

I suppose you will begin to think that I have forgotten you for not writing sooner but I have been pretty busy for the last two weeks marching and one thing and another and the prospect is that we will keep it up all winter or else gobble up Hood and his army and I think we have begun pretty well but I suppose you will get more news out of the papers about it than I can write you. Our Battery was not in the fight but we were close up where we could see it all and once in a while a shot would come over our heads but none of the boys were hurt. We are now about 36 miles from Nashville on the road to Columbia. We are waiting to have a bridge built over a creek and then we will move on again. I received two letters from you since I last wrote. We are having some of the worst weather here that I ever saw. It rains or snow every day and the wind is awful. The boys in the Battery are all well and I never felt better. I will not write a very long letter this time for it is so cold that I am almost froze now. As it is near Christmas and a Happy New Year and I hope by next Christmas I will be at home. I will close by asking you to write soon to your big son.

John Rieley

P.S. Direct the same as before.

Camp near Nashville, Ten.
January 11, 1865

Dear Mother:

I received your letter of December 24ᵗʰ a few days ago and was much pleased to hear from home.

We reached this place a few days ago. We leave again tomorrow for the Tennessee River, somewhere in the vicinity of Tuscumbia, Ala. When I reach our destination, I will write. If you do not hear from me in a couple of weeks, you must not get anxious on my account, as I do not expect that I will have a chance to write for some time.

I send two more photo with this letter. The weather was very cold on our march from Louisville to this place, but we got along very well and I was never in better health. There is a man belonging to our Company named John Schwab. If you have time and would like to, you might go and see him. I think that he is in the hospital in the Heights.

Direct your letters to Nashville.

Write soon,

Frank Rieley

Havana

On Board the Steamer

Cincinnati, Jan. 23rd

Dear Mother:

I received your most welcome letter of Jan. 2nd a few days since and was much pleased to hear from home again and to hear that you were all well. The last letter I wrote home I was near Columbia, Tennessee. We left there a few days after and went to Columbia. We left Columbia Jan. 2nd and went to Clifton on the Tennessee River and while laying there we got orders to load on steam boats to Louisville where we arrived on the 20th. We did not stay there only about an hour so I did not have much of a chance to see the city. We are having a pretty long ride of it this time. We have come 700 miles since I last wrote home and our journey is not half over yet for we are going to Grant or Sherman. The 30th of Dec. I got a crick in my back and I could not stand up for three days but it is all right again. I got it by lifting the end of a log we were getting for fire wood. We might have had a nice trip coming up here if the weather had been fine but it was cold and showing most of the time and we had to lay over three times on account of the fog, it was so thick that we could not see either side of the river. I will not write a very long letter this time as we are not going to stop here but a short time just long enough to get coal and rations. We are going up the river on this boat and I think we will get off at Parkersburg, Va and then go by rail to some place on the coast and then take boats to Grant or Sherman. All of the 23rd Corps is along. Tell Sylvester that I am glad to see that he remembers me yet and I will send him something from the War one of these days. I don't think I will have a chance to write again until we get on the coast and then I will try to give you a longer letter. Direct your next to Washington, D.C.

Yours in haste,

John Rieley

Camp near Gravelly Springs
Tenn. River, Ala.
February 8, 1865

Dear Mother:

I received your welcome letter of January 17ᵗʰ about a week ago, but did not have an opportunity of answering it before.

We have gone into Winter quarters here and expect to stay here two months. We have built log houses and have fireplaces in them and they are very comfortable. We are building stables for the horses.

Rations are rather scarce however, but we expect to have plenty in a few days.

I received a letter from John Schwab that fellow who is in the hospital in Cleveland a few days go. I have nothing very interesting to write and I might as well come to a close.

Please let me know in your next letter how much money I have sent home since I have been in the army.

Write soon and direct your letters to Eastport, Miss.

Frank Rieley

Washington

Dear Mother:

As we are going to march in the morning I thought I would write you a few lines this morning. We expect to go to Wilmington, North Carolina for there is part of the Corps there (or I would say near there for the rebels hold Wilmington yet). We would have gone there before but the weather ahs been so cold here that it has kept the river frozen up all the time since we have been here. I suppose you wanted to see my pretty bad from what they boys told me when they came back to the Battery and I have been sorry ever since they came back to the Battery and I didn't go home. They got to the Battery the same night that they left Cleveland which was the 30th of Jan. and we had the Battery loaded on the cars and was on ourselves and we started give minutes after they got there but if we had stayed there until morning I would have gone home and stayed 10 or 12 days. I have been sorry ever since that I did not wait until morning and then go home for we were in Wheeling only 150 miles from Cleveland. Captain Wilson never said a word to any of the boys that went home and there was over 30 of them home from the Battery. I sent home 50 dollars with some John Bissell sent to his father by express. I suppose he will draw it and hand it to you. I received that tobacco and the letter you wrote before the boys got home a few days since. I would have written sooner but I have been trying to get a pass to town to go through the Capital and I thought I would have something to write about but as it is I suppose I will have to write a short letter and won't get to see the Capital either. John Bissell has not been very well for a few days and he thinks he will be left here tomorrow if move. He has been having a bad cold and his face is swelled up pretty big. Some think he has got the mumps but the Doctor says not and he will be all right in a few days. He Is not very bad for he is running around camp all the time. I will keep this until morning and maybe we won't move and if we do I will let you know.

John Rieley

P.S. We are all loaded on the boat and expect to leave today the 18th. John Bissell is going with us. He is some better.

Dear Mother:

As I have a little spare time, I thought I would improve it in writing a few lines to you and let you know how I am getting along.

It is a long time since I have had a letter from you. The last one was dated the 17ᵗʰ almost two months ago and I am getting somewhat anxious to hear from home.

Everything goes on a usual here in the army. We have laid in our present quarters about six weeks and have pretty comfortable quarters. How much longer we will stay here, I cannot tell, but I suppose until Spring opens which will not be very long. We have had a great deal of rain the last week, regular showers like we have at home. We get rations and forage by steamboat on the Tenn. River which is only one mile from our camp. There are two divisions of cavalry camped at this place, but no infantry nearer than Eastport, Miss. twelve miles from here but across the river.

I see by the papers that General Sherman is raising the "Old Harry" with the rebels in South Carolina and having things pretty much his own way.

Direct letters to Eastport, Miss.

Frank

Camp near Kingston, N.C.
March 17, 1865

Dear Mother,

I received your most welcome letter of Feb. 22nd a few days since and was very glad to hear from home again and to hear that you are all well. We left Washington on Feb. 17th and went across the river to Alexandria and remained there one night and then run down the Potomac to Chesapeak Bay and then down the Bay to Fort Morris where we stopped overnight and then started on the Big Pond. We had first rate weather the whole trip. We stopped one night at Beaufort and got to Fort Fisher on the 22nd of Feb. the same day that Wilmington was taken. We stopped there two nights and then run up the Cape Fear River to Wilmington. We had a first rate trip. Some of the boys were sea sick and we lost one horse. He died on the boat. The sea sick-ness did not bother me any. We left Wilmington on the 6th of this month and started on one of the worst marches we have ever made for it was through a part of the state (N.C.) which is all under ground for it is most all swamps and quick sand. Sometimes we had to dig the horses out and there was one lace where we had to cross a creek and the rebels had burned the posts under the bridge and the bridge most so that when we would cross with our teams they would drop through and it worked first rate too for one of our teams dropped through and into the creek and if the guns had gone one inch farther it would have dropped right in on top of the team. Adam Liebe was one of the riders that went into the creek but he came out all right. There was not a man or a horse hurt but we had to cut the harness to get the horse out. Maybe you won't have any idea where Kingston is. It is about 100 miles Wilmington and 60 or 70 miles from Beaufort or Newberne. If you look on the map you can find the place. I don't know how long we will stop here but I don't think it will be long. When we leave here we will join Sherman and move on toward Richmond then I think we will make old Lee run into his hole or that last ditch that the war has been talking about so long. Part of our Corps had a pretty hard fight before we got up. I suppose you will see an account of it in the papers. While they was fighting here we were stuck in a cypress swamp 25 miles from here. All the boys are well and I never felt better.

John Rieley

141

Nashville, Tenn.
April 1, 1865

Dear Mother:

You will perhaps surprised to hear that I am in Nashville but such is the case.

While I was with the regiment at Eastport Miss., I was detailed by the Colonel to go to Louisville, Ky. with the overcoats and extra blankets of the regiment and express them home from that place.

Every man in the regiment had to send his overcoat home or destroy it. They have started on a big raid down through Alabama under command of General Wilson. Before starting they were ordered to dispose of everything not absolutely needed and therefor had to send extra blankets and overcoats to Louisville to be expressed home and I was sent with them.

I came from Eastport to this place by steamboat. I will have to stay here two or three days and then go to Louisville. It is a very long time since I got a letter from home and am anxious to hear if the folks are all well.

I need some money badly and I wish you would send me thirty dollars as soon as you get this letter. Send it by express to Louisville, Ky.

Frank Rieley

Sent it by Adams Express and write me as soon as you sent it. I expect to stay in Louisville a week.

FR

(On April 9, 1865, General Robert E. Lee, Head of the Confederate forces, surrendered at Appomattox, Virginia, ending the Civil War)

Nashville, Tenn.
April 17, 1865

Dear Mother:

I received your welcome letter of the 6ᵗʰ a few days ago and was very glad indeed to hear from home once more. I also received the money you sent me. I needed the money very badly or I would not have sent for it. We have not been paid since last November and I don't expect we will be paid until next Fall.

I am in camp at the cavalry department opposite Nashville and when you answer this letter, direct as follows: F. Rieley, Box 22 Edgefield Tenn.

The regiment is way down in Alabama under General Wilson and I do not expect to join them for some time. I think the fighting part of the war is over, but we may have to stay in the service some time longer perhaps until next Fall or Winter.

That was a sad thing the death of the President, but it cannot be helped now. Here in Nashville, they had made great preparations for celebrating the 15ᵗʰ, in honor of recent great victories of General Grant, before they had fairly got started, the news came of the president being killed, and every face which looked bright and joyous before turned to sadness.

Whilst I was in Louisville, I expressed home my overcoat and blankets by Adams Express Co. I could not get a box, so I put them in a bag. If you have not got them yet, go to Adams Express office an they will find them there.

Give my love to all the family and tell them I expect to be home soon. Don't forget the directions,

F. Rieley
Box 22, Edgefield, Tenn.

Raleigh, N.C., April 28, 1865

Dear Mother:

I received your welcome letter of April 7ᵗʰ a few days ago and was very glad to hear from home again. I would have written as soon as I received your letter but I have been waiting to see if I could not find out something about going home but it has been found out that our Corps will stay in this state some time yet. Perhaps until our time is out. I did think until yesterday that I would be at home next 4ᵗʰ of July or sooner but it is played out now. General Schofield has command of the Department of N.C. and the 23ʳᵈ Corps of his old Corps and he is going to keep them here until he gest things fixed up and the State back into the Union again and I think it will take until our time out or very near it. When I last wrote we were laying at Kinston. From there we moved to Goldsboro and camped there two days until Sherman's Army came in and then we went back to Mosley Hall, a small place on the rail road about half way between Goldsboro and Kinston. We camped there two or three weeks until Sherman's Army was well equipped and clothed and then we started for this place and I suppose you heard of our taking Raleigh long ago. We have been camped here two weeks today and it has been the dullest two weeks that I ever saw for I have been expecting every day to start for home the next and then after all to have to stay our time out it makes it come down pretty heavy. When you write again I wish you would let me know if Frank is with his Regiment. I got a letter from him a few days ago but it was written last winter so I thought I wouldn't answer it until I knew where he was. You told me in your last that he was in Nashville. The Brooklyn boys are all well and so am I. I don't suppose it is any use to tell you that Johnaron[49] has surrendered for you will see it in the papers long before this reaches you although he only surrendered yesterday. As news is scarce I will have to close asking you to write soon.

John Rieley

---

[49] An apparent mis-spelling of Johnston. General Joseph E. Johnston surrendered to General W.T. Sherman on April 26, 1865, just over two weeks after Lee had surrendered to Grant. Although the latter tends to get more attention, Johnston actually surrendered more troops than did Lee, having at the time under his command the Army of Tennessee, and the Department of Tennessee and Georgia, the Department of South Carolina, Georgia and Florida, and the Department of North Carolina and Southern Virginia, in all some 30,000 troops; Lee surrendered just under 28,000.

May 15, 1865
Edgefield, Tenn.

Dear Mother:

I was over town the other day and saw H. Englehorn who is discharged from the service and going home and I thought I would send a few lines with him.

I am as well as usual which is about all the news I have to write. My regiment is at Macon, Ga. at last accounts. How long they will stay there I don't know. I will return to the regiment as soon as an opportunity offers which will not be very soon according to present appearances as there is no railroad open yet to Macon. I understand the railroad will be opened in about a month and then I will return to the regiment. It is very warm and uncomfortable here at present.

I received your letter of April 27th and answered some time ago. Give my love to all and write soon. Direct as before.

F. Rieley

June 1, 1865
Edgefield, Tenn.

Dear Mother:

I am about to leave this place for the regiment and thought I would write and let you know before starting. I have not received an answer to your last two letters, one I sent by H. Englehorn about ten days ago. Your letter of April 23rd is the last. I hope that you are all well. Write as soon as you get this and direct to the regiment. The regiment is now at Macon, Ga. As soon as I get to the regiment, I will write again. I think we will be home by October or sooner.

I go by the railroad to Kingston and from there to Atlanta by wagon and from Atlanta to Macon by railroad.

Give my love to all,

Your son,

Frank Rieley

Dear Mother and Sister

As we are going to march in the morning I thought I would write you a few lines. We start at 5 o'clock. We go to Somerset, Kentucky. We were paid off yesterday for two months and I am going to send fifteen dollars home in this letter. We had quite an excitement in camp today. The other night Lieutenant Wilson gave a pass to ten men to go to church and four or five other men went along with them. Wilson was drunk and he saw them going and he sent a Sargent after them. I was down to the spring along with two other boys and came back with them and he put us all on extra duty. That night some one cut the hair all off this horse's neck which made him pretty mad. Today Captain Shields gave the boys liberty to go to town. Wilson went to town too and came back pretty drunk and he got a pistol and went around the camp hunting for a Corporal Brown (whom he thought cut the hair off his horse). He wanted to shoot him. Brown went down to head quarters and reported him and I think his time is pretty near our in the Battery. I have not got time to give you the particulars this time. Why in the world don't you write? Write soon.

John Rieley

Camp near Macon
June 11, 1865

Dear Mother:

I arrived here a few days ago safe and sound and am now with the regiment in this place. How long we will stay here I do not know but I guess we will stay until we start for home which will be in two or three months yet.

There are three regiments camped at this place besides ours, all Cavalry. Macon is a pretty fine town and has not been much disturbed by the war. Our cavalry division having been the first "Yankees" to enter the place. There are several railroads running from here one to Savannah, one to Augusta, one to Atlanta and one to Columbus and they are all in operation. The same men running them for us, that were running them for the rebels. I came from Nashville all the way except about thirty miles between Chattanooga and Atlanta where the railroad is not repaired yet, which I had to walk. The railroad will soon be repaired and then the cars will run all the way from Nashville to this place. The rebels down this way seem to be well satisfied with the new order of things and doing all in their power to uphold law and order. They have got their fill of war and are anxious to have the good old times of peace return as soon as possible.

It was near this place that Jeff David was captured.

The 4th Michigan Cavalry was the regiment that captured him belongs to our brigade. Our regiment was also in pursuit of him at the time but the 4th Michigan was sent out two days before our regiment came out. It is dreadfully warm but I guess I can stand it.

I have not received any answers to my last three or four letters. Have you received them? I left word with one of our boys who staid in Nashville to send on my letters to the regiment after I left.

I suppose John is home by this time.

From your son,

F. Rieley

Milledgeville, Ga.
July 6, 1865

Dear Mother:

I received your letter of June 6th a few days ago and would have answered it sooner but I thought I would wait until after the 4th of July. Our Company was sent to this place from Macon about two weeks ago. There are no other troops at this place except our Company. We are having fine times there.

Milledgeville is the capital of Georgia and has around two thousand inhabitants and is as the citizens say the healthiest place in Georgia. The citizens are all quiet and seem well disposed toward us. The only fault we have to find with the place is that it is dreadfully hot weather at present. How long we will stay here I can't say probably two or three months. The citizens of this place got us up a fine dinner on the 4th. I expect that you had a great time of it in Cleveland.

We are all anxious to be discharged and get home, and I hope that the time is not far off when we can leave Georgia.

We have not been paid off since we were at Louisville last November and all the boys would like to take a look at the greenbacks once more. I have heard that we will be paid a week after next, but I don't know how true it is.

The citizens are having great times with their negroes. The negroes won't work without their masters paying them. The masters won't pay them but turn them off the plantation, then the negroes come to the Yankees and then we send them back to their masters. The negroes have to work and the masters have to pay them. The negroes are our best friends here and everywhere through the South. Things are all turned upside down. There is no government and no one to keep the negroes from murdering one another except the "Yankees" as the people call us. In fact, if it was not for fear of the Yankees, the rebel soldiers and citizens would go on fighting one another and between the rebel soldiers, citizens and negroes, the old Harry would be to pay.

Give my best respects to all and my love to the family and write soon.

Yours son,

Frank Rieley

Milledgeville, Ga.
July 15, 1865

Dear Brother John:

I received your welcome letter of the 5ᵗʰ yesterday. I am glad to hear that you are out of the service and a loyal citizen of the United States.

I am very sorry that I was not at home on the 4ᵗʰ of July to enjoy the good old times.

I expect that our regiment will get out of the service some time next Fall.

There are no other troops at this place, only our Company and we are having pretty fine times. The citizens of this place got us up a dinner on the 4ᵗʰ. A first rate dinner for Georgia.

The people are having a great deal of trouble with the negroes. The negroes won't work without pay, the masters won't pay but turn them off the plantation, then the negroes come to the Yankees and then we send word to the masters to pay them. Milledgeville is a one horse town for a capital.

Give my love to all the family,

Yours truly,

Frank Rieley

Edgefield, Tenn.
August 4th, 1865

Dear Mother:

I received your letter of the 29th of July yesterday and was glad to hear from home once more.

I have nothing interesting to write except that we started from Macon on the 25th of lst month for this place to be mustered out of service. We reached here in safety on the 28th and expect to be mustered out of service tomorrow and start for Ohio the next day. I do not think that we will go to Cleveland to be paid off, we will I understand go to Columbus, Ohio and be paid off there and receive our final discharge. I expect to be home by the 15th of August.

You spoke of John Dorety in your last letter, and said you wish we were acquainted. We have been acquainted for nearly a year. He is a pretty fine fellow.

Give my love to all the family,

Yours truly,

Francis Rieley

Frank Rieley

John Rieley

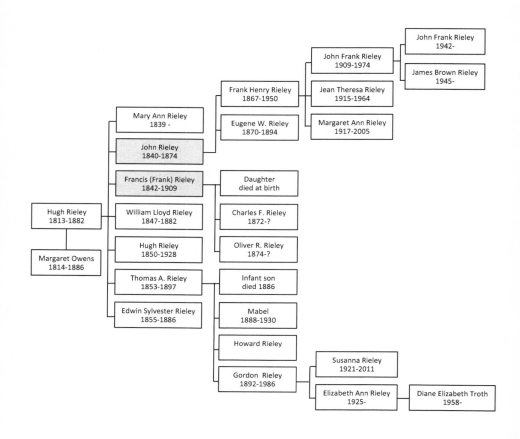

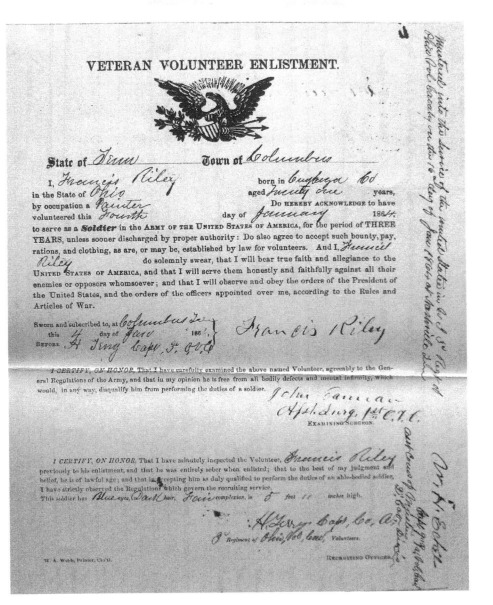

The volunteer enlistment document for Frank Rieley

Company Muster Rolls for Frank Rieley

Company Muster Rolls for John Rieley

Various Muster Roll documents for Frank Rieley

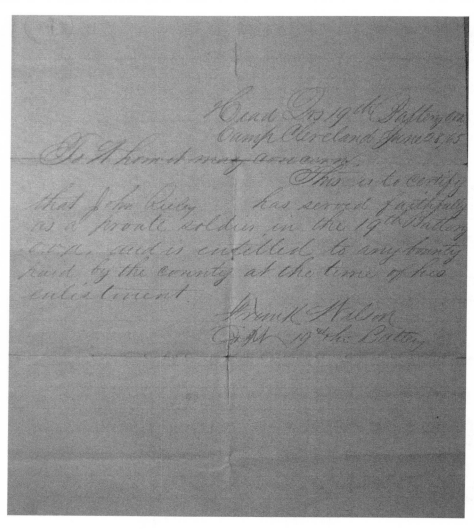

Document stating John Rieley's service during the Civil War

19th Ohio Battery reunion pendants

Wednesday Evening Sept 4th '61

Mr Graham,

Sir

Having heard that you and
Mr Clark advised Frank to go and enlist
I should like to have you let us know if you
can where he is. No doubt if you were interested
in his going away you were also enough interested
in his welfare that you ascertained, where
he went and in what regiment and company
he has enlisted. After having advised him
to go it is quite likely he would confide in you
that much that he would tell you of his
whereabouts. Of course I would not wish to censure
you in the least if you are not to blame but

First page of a letter written by Frank Rieley's mother regarding his
enlistment

162

if Frank was controlled by what you said to him in regard to his being so suitable a young man you ought to have consulted whether his mother was willing first and not begin to praise him and advise him to go. I supposed he was taught at Sabbath school to obey God's laws in preference to any other and had he learned them he would know that one was to obey his parents and I think you as professing Christian men ought not to persuade him to break them. I have reared Frank with as much care for him as Mrs Clark has her son and it is just as hard for me to part with him as for her to part with George or as it would be for your mother to see you or your brother go off to be engaged in the act of taking other men's lives and sending poor souls into eternity perhaps unprepared to meet the living God. If that is what your Sabbath

Second page of a letter written by Frank Rieley's mother regarding his enlistment

school teacher I think it high time
to with draw my other boys from it
that they may not in _Sabbath school_
at least be taught such principles.

Frank has for so far been an obedient
and good boy and had he obeyed his
own impulses he would I think never
have left home in the manner in which
he did. He had not told us he was going
or enlisted or any thing of the kind and
we have been to every camp and place
around town where he would be likely
to stay but could find nothing of him
and if you know where he is you will
confer a favor by letting us know.

Mrs. M. Rieley.

Third page of a letter written by Frank Rieley's mother regarding his
enlistment

Wednesday evening, Sept. 4th,

Wednesday evening, Sept. 4th,

1861

Mr. Graham,

Sir

Having heard that you and Mr. Clark advised Frank to go and enlist I should like to have you let us know if you can where he is. No doubt if you were interested in his going away you were also enough interested where he went and in what regiment and company he has enlisted. After having advised him to go it is quite likely he would confide in you that much that he would tell you of his whereabouts. Of course I would not wish to concern you in the least if you are not to blame but if Frank was controlled by what you said to him in regard to his being so suitable a young man you ought to have consulted whether his mother was willing first and not begin to praise him and advise him to go.

I supposed he was taught at Sabbath school to obey God's laws in preference to any others and had he learned them he would know that one was to obey his parents and I think you as professing Christian men ought not to persuade him to break these. I have reared Frank with as much care for him as Mrs. Clark has her son and it is just as hard for me to part with him as for her to part with George or as it should be for your mother to see you or your brother go off to be engaged in this act of taking other men's lives and sending poor souls into eternity perhaps unprepared to meet the living God. If that is what your Sabbath school teaches I think it high time to with draw my other boys from it that they may not in Sabbath school at least be taught such principles.

Frank has for so far been our obedient and good boy and had he obeyed his own impulses he would I think never have left home in the manner in which he did. He had not told us he was going or enlisted or anything of this kind and we have been to every camp and place around town where he would be likely to stay but could find nothing of him and if you know where he is you will confer a favour by letting us know.

Mrs. M. Rieley

From Wikipedia:

"Frederick Henry Dyer (July 2, 1849 – September 21, 1917) served as a drummer boy in the Union Army during the American Civil War. After the war, he wrote *A Compendium of the War of the Rebellion* – a complete record of every regiment formed under the Union Army, their histories, and the battles they fought in – taking forty years to compile."

From Dyer's Compendium of the War of the Rebellion:

The 3ʳᵈ Ohio Volunteer Cavalry War Record

3rd Regiment Cavalry. Organized at Camp Worcester September 4-December 11, 1861. Moved to Camp Dennison, near Cincinnati, Ohio, January 14, 1862, and to Jeffersonville, Ind., February 21. Moved to Nashville, Tenn., March 2. Attached to 6th Division, Army Ohio, to June, 1862. Cavalry Brigade, Army Ohio, to September, 1862. 2nd Brigade, Cavalry Division, Army Ohio, to November, 1862. 2nd Brigade, Cavalry Division, Army of the Cumberland, to January, 1863. 2nd Brigade, 1st Cavalry Division, Army Cumberland, to March, 1863. 2nd Brigade, 2nd Cavalry Division, Army of the Cumberland, to October, 1864. 2nd Brigade, 2nd Division, Wilson's Cavalry Corps, Military Division Mississippi, to August, 1865.

SERVICE.--March with 6th Division, Army Ohio, from Nashville to Savannah, Tenn., March 29-April 6, 1862. Action at Lawrenceburg April 4 (1st Battalion). Advance on and siege of Corinth, Miss., April 29-May 30. Guard duty along Memphis & Charleston Railroad June to August. Near Woodville, Ala., August 4. Expedition from Woodville to Guntersville, Ala. (3rd Battalion). Guntersville and Law's Landing August 28 (3rd Battalion). Expedition to Dunlap August 29-31. Old Deposit Ferry August 29 (3rd Battalion). March to Louisville, Ky., in pursuit of Bragg September 3-25. Glasgow, Ky., September 18. Munfordsville September 20-21 (1st Battalion). Pursuit of Bragg into Kentucky October 1-15. Bardstown Pike October 1. Near Bardstown October 4. Battle of Perryville October 8. Lexington October 17-18. Pursuit of Morgan to Gallatin, Tenn. March to Nashville, Tenn., and duty there till December 26. Tunnel Hill November 19. Advance on Murfreesboro December 26-30. Franklin December 26-27. Battle of Stone's River December 30-31, 1862, and January 1-3, 1863. Overall's Creek December 31. Stewart's Creek and Lavergne January 1, 1863. Conduct trains to Nashville and return. Insane Asylum January 3. Shelbyville Pike January 5. Near Woodbury January 19 (Cos. "A," "D," "E" and "F"). Bradysville Pike, near Murfreesboro, January 23. Expedition to Liberty, Auburn and Alexandria February 3-5. Vaught's Hill, Milton, February 18. Bradysville

March 1. Expedition toward Columbia March 4-14. Chapel Hill March 5. Rutherford Creek March 10-11. Woodbury Pike March 27 (2nd Battalion). Expedition from Readyville to Woodbury April 2 (2nd Battalion). Smith's Ford April 2. Expedition from Murfreesboro to Auburn, Snow Hill, Liberty, etc., April 2-6. Snow Hill, Woodbury, April 3. Liberty April 3. Franklin April 9-10. Schoeppe House May 9. Reconnoissance from Lavergne May 12. Middleton May 21-22. Scout to Smithville June 4-5. Snow Hill June 4. Smithville June 5. Middle Tennessee or Tullahoma Campaign June 23-July 7. Morris Ford, Elk River, July 2. Occupation of Middle Tennessee till August 16. Expedition to Huntsville July 13-22. Passage of Cumberland Mountains and Tennessee River, and Chickamauga (Ga.) Campaign August 16-September 22. Reconnoissance from Stevenson to Trenton, Ga., August 28-31. Reconnoissance from Winston's Gap to Broomtown Valley September 5. Alpine September 3 and 8. Reconnoissance from Alpine to Lafayette September 10. Battle of Chickamauga, Ga., September 19-21. Operations against Wheeler and Roddy September 30-October 17. McMinnville October 4. Garrison's Creek, near Fosterville, October 6 (1st Battalion). Wartrace October 6 (1st Battalion). Farmington October 7. Sim's Farm, near Shelbyville, October 7. Chattanooga-Ringgold Campaign November 23-27. Raid on East Tennessee & Georgia Railroad November 24-27. Charleston November 26. Cleveland November 27. March to relief of Knoxville November 28-December 8. Near Loudoun December 2. Philadelphia December 3. Expedition to Murphey, N. C., December 6-11. Regiment reenlisted January, 1864. Demonstration on Dalton, Ga., February 22-27. Near Dalton February 23. Tunnel Hill, Buzzard's Roost Gap and Rocky Faced Ridge February 23-25. Atlanta (Ga.) Campaign May 1-September 8. Courtland Road, Ala., May 26. Pond Springs, near Courtland, May 27. Moulton May 28-29. Operations about Marietta and against Kenesaw Mountain June 10-July 1. Rosswell June 10. McAffee's Cross Roads June 11. Noonday Creek June 15-19 and 27. Powder Springs June 20. Near Marietta June 23. Assault on Kenesaw June 27. Nickajack Creek July 2-5. Big Shanty June 3. Rottenwood Creek July 4. On line of the Chattahoochie River July 5-17. Garrard's Raid to Covington July 22-24. Covington July 22. Siege of Atlanta July 24-August 15. Garrard's Raid to South River July 27-31. Flat Rock Bridge July 28. Peach Tree Road August 15. Kilpatrick's Raid around Atlanta August 18-22. Red Oak, Flint River and Jonesborough August 19. Lovejoy Station August 20. Jonesborough August 22. Operations at Chattahoochie River Bridge August 26-September 2. Occupation of Atlanta September 2. Florence September 17. Operations against Hood and Forest in North Georgia and North Alabama September 29-November 3. Near Lost Mountain October 4-7. New Hope Church October 5. Dallas October 7. Rome October 10-11. Narrows October 11. Coosaville Road, near Rome, October 13. Near Summerville October 18. Little River, Ala., October 20. Leesburg and Blue Pond October 21. King's Hill, near Gadsden, Ala., October 23. Ladiga, Terrapin Creek, October 28. Ordered to Louisville, Ky., and duty there till December. Ordered to Gravelly Springs, Ala., December 28, and duty there till March, 1865. Wilson's Raid to Macon, Ga., March 22-April 24. Selma April 2. Montgomery April 12. Pleasant Hill April 18. Double Bridges, Flint River, April 18. Macon, Ga.,

April 20. Duty at Macon and in Dept. of Georgia till August. Mustered out August 14, 1865. Regiment lost during service 1 Officer and 58 Enlisted men killed and mortally wounded and 6 Officers and 229 Enlisted men by disease. Total 294.

The 19th Ohio Light Infantry War Record

19th Regiment Infantry (3 Months). Organized at Cleveland, Ohio, April and May, 1861. Moved to Columbus, Ohio, May 27 and mustered in May 29, to date from April 27, 1861. Companies "A" and "B" moved to Bellaire, Ohio, May 27, and guard duty there till June 3, and at Glover's Gap and Manington till June 20. Regiment at Zanesville, Ohio till June 20. Moved to Parkersburg, W. Va., June 20-23. Attached to Rosecran's Brigade, Army of West Virginia. Moved to Clarksburg June 25. March to Buckhannon June 29-30. Occupation of Buckhannon June 30. Campaign in West Virginia July 6-17. Battle of Rich Mountain July 11. Moved to Columbus, Ohio, July 23-27. Mustered out by Companies: "A" August 27, "B" and "C" August 29, "D" August 30, "E" August 28, "F" August 30, "G" August 31, "H" August 18, "I" August 30, "K" August 31, 1861. 19th Regiment Infantry (3 Years). Organized at Alliance, Ohio, September 25, 1861. Moved to Camp Dennison, Ohio, November 6, thence to Louisville, Ky., November 16. Attached to 11th Brigade, Army of the Ohio, to December, 1861. 11th Brigade, 1st Division, Army of the Ohio, to March, 1862. 11th Brigade, 5th Division, Army of the Ohio, to September, 1862. 11th Brigade, 5th Division, 2nd Corps, Army of the Ohio, to November, 1862. 1st Brigade, 3rd Division, Left Wing 14th Army Corps, Army of the Cumberland, to January, 1863. 1st Brigade, 3rd Division, 21st Army Corps, Army of the Cumberland, to October, 1863. 3rd Brigade, 3rd Division, 4th Army Corps, to June, 1865. 2nd Brigade, 3rd Division, 4th Army Corps, to August, 1865. Dept. of Texas, to October, 1865.

SERVICE.--Duty at Camp Jenkins, Louisville, Lebanon, Renick's Creek, Jamestown and Greasy Creek till February, 1862. March to Nashville, Tenn., February 15-March 8, and to Savannah, Tenn., March 18-April 6. Battle of Shiloh, Tenn., April 6-7, Advance on and siege of Corinth, Miss., April 29-May 30. Pursuit to Booneville May 31-June 6. Buell's Campaign in North Alabama and Middle Tennessee June to August. March to Battle Creek, Ala., and duty there till August 21. March to Louisville, Ky., in pursuit of Bragg August 21-September 26. Pursuit of Bragg into Kentucky October 1-15. Battle of Perryville, Ky., October 8 (Reserve). March to Nashville, Tenn., October 16-November 7, and duty there till December 26. Advance on Murfreesboro, Tenn., December 26-30. Battle of Stone's River December 30-31, and January 1-3, 1863. Duty at Murfreesboro till June. Middle Tennessee or Tullahoma Campaign June 22-July 7. Liberty Gap June 22-24. At McMinnville till August 16. Passage of the Cumberland Mountains and Tennessee River and Chickamauga (Ga.) Campaign August 16-September 22. Battle of Chickamauga September 19-20. Siege of Chattanooga, Tenn., September 24-November 23. Chattanooga-Ringgold Campaign November 23-27. Orchard Knob November 23-24. Mission Ridge November 25. Pursuit to Graysville November 26-27. March to relief of Knoxville November 28-December 8. Operations in East Tennessee December, 1863, to April, 1864. Regiment reenlisted January 1, 1864. Atlanta (Ga.) Campaign May 1-September 8, Duty at Parker's Gap May 6-18. Advance to the Etowah May 18-23. Cassville May 19. Advance on Dallas May 22-25. Operations on Pumpkin Vine Creek and battles about Dallas, New Hope Church and Allatoona Hills May 25-June 5. Pickett's Mills May 27. Operations about Marietta and against Kenesaw Mountain June 10-July 2. Pine Mountain June 11-14. Lost Mountain June 15-17. Assault on Kenesaw June 27. Ruff's Station July 4. Chattahoochie River July 5-17. Peach Tree Creek July 19-20. Siege of Atlanta July 22-August 25. Flank movement on Jonesboro August 25-30. Battle of Jonesboro August 31-September 1. Lovejoy Station September 2-6. Operations against Hood, in North Georgia and North Alabama September 29-November 3. Nashville Campaign November-December. Columbia, Duck River, November 24-27. Battle of Franklin November 30. Battle of Nashville December 15-16. Pursuit of Hood to the Tennessee River December 17-28. Moved to Huntsville, Ala., and duty there till March, 1865. Expedition from Whitesburg February 17. Operations in East Tennessee March 15-April 22. Duty at Nashville till June. Moved to New Orleans, La., June 16, thence to Texas. Duty at Green Lake till September 11, and at San Antonio till October 21. Mustered out October 24, 1865. Regiment lost during service 7 Officers and 104 Enlisted men killed and mortally wounded and 6 Officers and 162 Enlisted men by disease. Total 279.

About the Author

James B. Rieley is a retired CEO who has written extensively on the subjects of realizing personal and collective organisational potential. He is the author of Gaming the System ((FT/Prentice Hall), Leadership (Hodder), Strategy and Performance (Hodder), Change and Crisis Management (Hodder), as well as being the publisher of Plain Talk about Business Performance. Rieley holds an earned Ph.D. in Organisational Effectiveness, and can be reached at jbrieley@rieley.com